HYMN TO
OLD AGE

HERMANN HESSE

HYMN TO OLD AGE

Translated from the German by
David Henry Wilson

PUSHKIN PRESS

LONDON

English translation © David Henry Wilson 2011
Original text © Suhrkamp Verlag Frankfurt am Main

Hymn to Old Age first published in German as
Mit der Reife wird man immer jünger in 1990.
This translation is of the revised 2002 edition.

This edition first published in 2011 by
Pushkin Press
71-75 Shelton Street
London WC2H 9JQ

ISBN 978 1 906548 32 2

Cover Illustration *The Four Ages of Man* Valentin de Boulogne
© National Gallery London/Bridgeman Art Library
Frontispiece *Hermann Hesse c1950* Martin Hesse
© Suhrkamp Verlag

Set in 11 on 14 Monotype Baskerville by Tetragon
Proudly printed and bound in Great Britain by TJ International,
Padstow, Cornwall on Munken Premium White 90gsm

www.pushkinpress.com

CONTENTS

*The titles in square brackets denote passages
taken from longer texts.*

HYMN TO
OLD AGE

A WALK IN THE SPRING

ONCE MORE THE LITTLE teardrops stand shining on the resinous leaf buds, the first peacock butterflies open and close their fine velvet cloaks, and boys play with spinning tops and marbles. It's Holy Week, filled to overflowing with sounds, charged with memories of dazzling coloured Easter eggs, Jesus in the Garden of Gethsemane, Jesus on Golgotha, the St Matthew Passion, youthful enthusiasms, first loves, first young taste of melancholy. Anemones nod in the moss, and buttercups glow warmly on the banks of streams.

On my lonely wanderings, I do not distinguish between the instincts and urges within me and the concert of growing things whose thousand voices encompass me from without. I have come from the city, where after a long absence I was once more among people, and I have sat in a train, seen pictures and sculptures and heard wonderful new songs by Othmar Schoeck. Now the joyful breeze brushes my face just as it caresses the nodding anemones, but as it whirls up a swarm of memories in me like a dust cloud, a reminder of pain and transience rises from my blood into my conscious mind. Stone on the path, you are stronger than me! Tree in the meadow, you will outlast me, and perhaps so will you, little raspberry bush, and perhaps even you, rose-scented anemone.

For a single breath I sense more profoundly than ever the transience of my form, and I feel drawn into transformation—to the stone, the earth, the raspberry bush, the tree root. My thirst is for the signs of passing, for the earth, the water and the withering of the leaves. Tomorrow, the day after, soon, soon I shall be you, I shall be leaves, I shall be earth, I shall be roots, I shall write no more words on paper, I shall no longer smell the regal wallflower, I shall no longer carry the dentist's bill around in my pocket, I shall no longer be pestered by menacing officials demanding proof of citizenship, and so—swim cloud in the blue, flow water in the brook, bud leaf on the bough, I have sunk into oblivion and into my thousand-times-longed-for transformation.

Ten and a hundred times more you will grasp me, enchant me and imprison me, world of words, world of opinions, world of people, world of increasing pleasure and feverish fear. A thousand times you will delight me and terrify me, with songs sung at the piano, with newspapers, with telegrams, with obituaries, with registration forms and with all your crazy odds and ends, you, world full of pleasure and fear, sweet opera full of melodic nonsense. But never more, may God grant, will you be completely lost to me, devotion to transience, passionate music of change, readiness for death, desire for rebirth. Easter will always return, pleasure will always become fear, fear will always become redemption, and the song of the past will accompany me on my way without grief, filled with affirmation, filled with readiness, filled with hope.

1920

WATCHING AND LISTENING

A sound so sweet, a breeze so shy—
Through grey of day they waft
Like birds' wings fluttering in the sky
Like scents of spring so soft.

Out of life's early morning hours
Come memories of yore
Like oceans spawning silver showers
That shine, then are no more.

Yesterday seems far from me
The long-gone past is near.
Magical prehistory
Is an open garden here.

Perhaps my ancestor awakes
From a thousand years of calm
And now with my own voice he speaks
And in my blood keeps warm.

Perhaps a messenger attends
And soon to me he'll come;
Perhaps before the long day ends
I'll be going home.

SUMMER'S END

IT WAS A FINE and shining summer here in the southern Alps, and for two weeks I had been feeling a secret fear that it would end—a fear that I know to be the additional and most secret ingredient of all things beautiful. Especially I feared even the faintest sign of a thunderstorm, because from mid-August onwards, any thunderstorm can easily get out of control, can last for days, and that means the end of summer, even if the weather manages to recover. Particularly here in the south it's almost the rule that summer's neck is broken by such a storm and that, blazing and quaking, it must fade and die. Then, when the day-long, violent shudders of this storm in the sky have ended, when the thousand flashes and the endless concerts of thunder and the raging torrents of lukewarm rain have passed away, one morning or afternoon there will emerge from the seething mass of clouds a cool calm sky, of serene colour, filled with autumn, and the shadows in the landscape will become a little sharper and blacker, having lost their colours but gained in form, like a fifty-year-old man who yesterday looked fit and fresh, but suddenly after an illness, a grief, a disappointment, has a face full of little lines, and in all the wrinkles lie the tiny signs of weathering. Such a final summer storm is terrible, and the death throes of summer are horrific, with its violent struggle against the compulsion to die, its crazed and agonised rage, its threshing and heaving, all of which is in vain and after a few more convulsions must end helplessly in extinction.

This year, it seems that summer is not undergoing such a wild, dramatic end (though it's still possible). This time it appears to be seeking a slow and gentle death by old age. There is nothing so characteristic of these days, and by no other signs do I sense so inwardly this special, infinitely beautiful kind of summer's end, as when coming home from a late-evening walk or from a country supper—bread, cheese and wine in a shaded inn somewhere in the forest. What is unique about such evenings is the dilation of warmth, the slow and imperceptible increase of coolness, the nocturnal dew and the silent, infinitely pliant retreat of summer even in its dying moments of resistance. When you walk for two or three hours after sunset, you can sense the struggle in a thousand fine waves. Then, in every dense thicket, every bush, every narrow pathway, the warmth of day has gathered itself and hidden away, holding on grimly for dear life throughout the night, clinging to any refuge, any shelter from the wind. At this hour, on the western side of the hills, the forests are great storage heaters, gnawed at from all sides by the cool night air, and not only every dip, every stream, but every woodland form, every thinness and thickness tells the wanderer with utmost clarity the changing degrees of heat. Just as a skier crossing a mountain landscape can sense each rise and fall, each lengthways and sideways ridge, simply through the bending of his knees, so that with a little practice his knees will give him a complete image of the mountain slope as he descends, I can read the image of the landscape in the darkness of a moonless night simply from the delicate waves of warmth. I enter a forest, and after just three steps I am enveloped in a rapidly increasing flow of heat, as if from a glowing stove, and I find that this heat expands and contracts according to the thickness of the vegetation; every dried-up stream, which has long since lost its water but still keeps a residue of damp in the earth, announces its presence by radiating its coolness. In every season the temperatures at differ- ent points of a landscape will vary, but only at this time when late summer turns into early autumn can one feel it so clearly and so strongly. As in winter the rose-red of the bare mountains, as in spring the teeming moistness of air and growing plants, as at the start of summer the nocturnal swarms of fireflies, so too at the end of summer this wonderful night-time walk through the changing waves of warmth is one of those sensual experiences that penetrate most deeply into one's mood and one's sense of being alive.

That's how it was last night when I walked home from the inn, and as I stepped onto the narrow path that leads to Sant'Abbondio Cemetery I was struck by the cool damp rising from the meadows and the lakeside valley. At the same time the comforting warmth of the forest that had shyly crept beneath the acacias, chestnuts and alders was still with me. How the forest fought against the autumn, how the summer fought against inevitable death! So too, in the years when his summer fades, does man fight against the withering and dying, against the penetrating cold of space, against the penetrating cold of his own blood. And so with renewed vigour he devotes himself to the little games and tiny sounds of life, to the thousand sweet delights of the earth's surface, to the showers of shimmering colours, the scurrying shadows of clouds, clinging with smiles and tremors of fear to the most ephemeral of things, seeing the approach of his own death and extracting both terror and comfort from it as he tremblingly learns the art of dying.

Here lies the frontier between youth and age. Some cross it at the age of forty or even sooner, and some do not notice it until late in their fifties or sixties. But the story is always the same—instead of the art of living we begin to study that other art; instead of shaping and refining our character, we begin to focus on its decline and fall—and suddenly, almost from one day to the next, we feel old, and the thoughts and interests and emotions of youth seem alien to us. It is during these times of transition that we may be transfixed and touched by such tiny, tender spectacles as the fading and dying of summer, which fills our hearts with wonderment and dread, and makes us tremble and smile.

The forest has lost its green of yesterday, and the vine leaves are beginning to turn yellow, while the grapes below are blue and purple. Towards evening, the mountains are violet and the sky has those hues of emerald that mean the approach of autumn. What then? Once again there will be no more evenings in the grotto, no more afternoons bathing in the lake at Agno, no more sitting painting under the chestnut trees. Lucky the man who can then go back to some meaningful work he loves, to people he loves, and to a home of his own. But he who does not have such things, and who has no illusions of such things, then creeps away from the approaching cold to hide in his bed, or escapes on his travels, and as a wanderer hither and thither watches those who have a home, who live in a community, who have faith in their occupations and professions, and watches them strain and struggle and strive, and beyond all their faith and all their endeavour he sees the slow, imperceptible approach of the cloud that is the next war, the next crisis, the next collapse, visible only to the idlers, the faithless, the disillusioned—to those who have grown old and whose lost optimism has given way to the tender predilection of age for bitter truths. We who are old see how day by day, beneath the waving banners of the optimists, the world becomes more perfect, how each nation feels more divine, more infallible, more justified in its use of force and its heedless aggression, how in art and sport and science new fashions and new stars shine forth, names go up in lights, superlatives drip from the newspapers, and we see how all this is pulsating with life, with warmth, with enthusiasm, with a passionate lust for life, with a drunken resistance to death. Wave upon wave of it glows like the waves of warmth in the summer forests of Ticino. Everlasting and powerful is the theatre of life, without substance, but forever in motion, forever doing battle with death.

There are still many good things ahead before winter takes over once more. The blueish grapes will become soft and sweet, young men will sing at harvest time, and young girls in their coloured headscarves will stand among the yellowing vines like lovely wild flowers in the field. There are still many good things ahead, and many things that seem bitter to us today will eventually seem sweet, once we have learnt to master the art of dying. Meanwhile, we wait for the grapes to ripen, for the chestnuts to fall, and we hope we shall still be there to enjoy the next full moon, and even though we are growing older and older, we see that death is still a long way away. As a poet once wrote—

> *A burgundy, a stove's warm breath*
> *For such delights we old folk pray*
> *And finally a gentle death*
> *But that's for later—not today!*

1926

GROWING OLD

The foolish things by youth desired—
Sword and helmet, silk ties, curls—
Were those to which I too aspired
Above all to impress the girls.

Only now, though, have I seen—
Old men like me, you'll understand,
No longer have such things to hand—
Only now, then, have I seen
How wise my youthful quest had been.
Gone are the silks and curly locks
Gone is all the glittering gold.
But in their place what I've paraded—
Wisdom, virtue, nice warm socks—
Alas will also soon have faded
And the earth is very cold.

A burgundy, a stove's warm breath
For such delights we old folk pray
And finally a gentle death
But that's for later—not today!

'Youth' is what remains of the child in us, and the more we have of it, the more richly we can partake of this cold-conscious life.

From a letter written in
1912 to Wilhelm Einsle

In childhood, how long it took from one birthday to the next! In old age, it goes faster and faster.

From a letter written in December
1960 to his son Bruno

In old age, one often experiences the paradox that while the years go by at incredible speed, the hours and days often pass very slowly.

From a letter written in
December 1949 to Otto Korradi

One ages so quickly if one is out of step with the world.

From a letter written on 21st October
1929 to Carlo Isenberg

As one grows older, one loves the autumn more and more, but one fears the spring.

From a letter written on
26th October 1929 to Elsy Bodmer

Growing old is like what Goethe said of loneliness—he who gives way to it will soon be alone. And he who gives way to old age will soon be old. Every evening the grey phantom stands beside the bed. But first I shall lash out a few times, and let off a few fireworks.

From a letter written in
January 1920 to Anni Bodmer

Grandparents, the old folk, who themselves are once more in the process of becoming children, do not take children seriously, just as they do not take themselves seriously. Pathos is a fine thing, and is often wonderful among young people. For older people, humour is more fitting—the smile, the self-irony, changing the

27

world into an image, seeing things as if they were the fleeting spectacle of evening clouds.

From Abendwolken
(Evening Clouds) *1926*

LATE SUMMER

Late summer still gives out its warmth so sweet
In daily gifts. Above the cups of flowers
With wings that seem more wearily to beat
A butterfly shines bright in golden showers.

The air of evening and the air of morning
Is warm and moist with drops of mist and dew
And from the mulberry tree, without a warning
A yellow leaf drifts off into the blue.

The shady vine leaves hide the purple grapes
A lizard lies upon the sunlit stone.
Under some magic spell the world now sleeps
And with its dreams it must be left alone.

Sometimes the endless golden stillness seems
Accompanied by music sweet and pleasant
Until the world awakens from its dreams
Returning to the living, breathing present.

We old ones stand and pluck fruit from the bough
With hands well warmed and summer-sun-burned brown.
The day still smiles, the sun has not gone down
And we still revel in the here and now.

THE OLD DAYS

IN MY HOMETOWN LIVES an old schoolteacher—one of the good ones—who writes to me once a year. He goes on living quietly and contemplatively in his little hermitage with garden, and when someone is buried in the town it's generally one of his former pupils. This old gentleman recently wrote to me again. And although I have a totally different opinion from his, and contradicted him vehemently in my response, nevertheless his views on the old days and the present seem to me well worth reading, and so I shall reproduce this extract from his letter. He writes—

… I can't help thinking that the present world is separated from that which still existed effectively in my youth by a greater gulf than that which normally separates the generations. I can't know it for sure, and history seems to teach us that my view is an error to which every ageing generation is prone. For the flow of progress is constant, and at all times the fathers are overtaken by the sons and can no longer

make themselves understood. And yet I cannot change my feeling that—at least in our nation and country—during the last few decades everything has changed much more radically, as if our history has accelerated far more swiftly than in former times.

Shall I tell you what seems to me the most fundamental aspect of this revolution in the Zeitgeist? In a nutshell, I sense a ubiquitous decline in respect and in modesty. I don't wish to sing the praises of the old days. I know that in every age there has been just a small proportion of good and useful things, one thinker for every thousand talkers, one true believer for every thousand of the soulless, one gentleman for every philistine. Perhaps basically there were no individual matters that were better then than now. But on the whole it seems to me that until a few decades ago there was in our general way of life more decency, more modesty than today. Now everything is done with far more noise and far more self-love, and the world resounds with the certainty that it stands on the threshold of a Golden Age, whereas in fact no one is happy.

All around people talk, preach and write about science, culture, beauty, personality! But awareness that all these valuable things can only thrive in silence and can only grow in the night seems to have disappeared completely. Every branch of knowledge and learning is in such a hurry to bear fruit immediately, and to see concrete and successful results.

Knowledge of a natural law, which in itself is such a sublime, internal event, is rushed with questionable haste into practice—as if one could accelerate the growth of a tree once one had fathomed out the law governing its growth. And so everywhere people are burrowing round the roots, experimenting and exploiting the work, and that makes me suspicious. Neither for scholars nor for poets is there anything left that people are prepared to remain silent about. Everything is discussed, laid bare, illuminated, and every study wishes immediately to take on the status of knowledge. A new fact, a new discovery has already been popularised and exploited by the newspapers even before the researcher has finished his work. And every little snippet of information gleaned by the anatomist or the zoologist immediately has the arts trembling with fear! A particular statistic influences the philosophers, a microscopic discovery changes the spiritual teaching of the theologists. And in no time you also have an author writing a novel about it. And those old, sacred questions about the roots of our existence are currently material for entertainment, affected and influenced by every breeze of fashion in the arts and sciences. There seems no longer to be any silence, any ability to wait, or any distinction between big and small.

That is how it is in visible daily life. Rules for living, health guidance, forms of houses and furniture and other items for long-term use which used to be endowed with a certain stability change as swiftly today as clothing fashions. Every year people have reached the peak of every subject—they've achieved the ultimate. In the lives of individual families it all leads to a great gulf between the inside and the outside, between the facade and the interior, and hence to a decline in ethics and in the art of living, whose basic feature is an astonishing lack of fantasy.

It seems to me almost as if this is the real disease of our time. Fantasy is the mother of contentment, of humour, of the art of living. And fantasy can only flourish on the foundations of an inner understanding between man and his material surroundings. These surroundings need not be beautiful, nor strange, nor charming. We just need the time to integrate with them, and that is what is missing everywhere today. Anyone who wears nothing but brand-new clothes which he has to change and renew as often as possible will thereby lose a piece of the ground on which fantasy rests. He doesn't know how alive, lovely, friendly, amusing, exciting and full of memories an old hat, an old pair of riding breeches, an old waistcoat can be. And it's the same with an old table and chair, a tried and trusted old cupboard, fire screen, bootjack. And the cup you've drunk from since childhood, grandfather's chest of drawers, the old clock!

Of course you don't have to go on living in the same place in the same rooms with the same objects. Someone *can live his whole life travelling and without a home and yet still be blessed with the richest imagination. But he too will certainly carry some favourite item around with him, from which he will never allow himself to be separated, even if it's only a ring, a pocket watch, an old knife or wallet.*

But I'm digressing. I just wanted to say that this hankering after change makes people poorer and does damage to the soul by encouraging dislike of stability, whether it be in one's world view or in one's household objects; it becomes difficult for children to write, create, cope with material things if they are confronted with an overabundance of toys and picture books. And it becomes difficult for adults to adhere to any belief, to hold on to any inner conviction if every stall can make things easily and cheaply available to them that should be acquired slowly and through their own dedication. Now everyone thinks he must grab hold of everything, and there is nothing easier for him than to switch from the Church to godlessness, from there to Darwin, from him to Buddha, and from him to Nietzsche or Haeckel or whoever else, without needing to make much effort or do much studying. It has become so easy to know without having to learn.

Of course this will not bring about the end of mankind. And of course today as always there are those good-hearted, hard-working folk who turn their backs on the easy ways and cheap successes. But it has become more difficult for them. As has life in general, in which the average level of culture both at home and at work has fallen. It may have seemed trivial and silly in the old days when many family men pursued their pleasant hobbies, when one played the flute, another practised calligraphy, or took watches to pieces and put them back together again, or made models out of paper and cardboard. But such things did no harm and people were happy. And even if for the genius, for the individual with great aspirations, an ever thirsty discontent is necessary and even beneficial, for the vast majority of lesser folk, contentment is no less necessary and no less beneficial if things are to remain in balance.

In former times families and even wider communities shared intimate memories, were attached to little things in the outside world which went on exerting a powerful inner influence and gave rise to a wonderful feeling of home. There was recognition of tiny connections which must have been dangerous for men of reason, but for men of fantasy was a source of inner relatedness and also a treasure trove for jokes and cheerfulness. There were so many 'characters', because people enjoyed little oddities and took note of them, and as this was the practice on all sides, it created a tone of merriment and goodwill in communication and conversation. Of course even today every real family has its own tone, its secrets, its forms of teasing and its own particular language, and that will always be the case. But beyond the confines of the family, for the most part modern societies lack such colour and cheerfulness, and this lack of contentment cannot be replaced by expensive clothes and meals …

This was what my old teacher wrote to me. As I said, I don't share all his views. But it seems to me he does have a point.

1907

FROM TIME TO TIME

When suddenly I find unfurled
A memory of childhood times
It's like some legendary world
Transfigured by a poet's rhymes.

In silence then my gaze must sink
Weighed down by times so bright and blessed
And I can only sit and think
Like one by heavy guilt oppressed.

ON A HEALTH CURE

S CARCELY HAD MY TRAIN arrived in Baden, and scarcely had I managed with some difficulty to climb down the carriage steps, when the magic of Baden revealed itself to me. Standing on the wet concrete platform, peering around for the hotel porter, I saw three or four fellow patients getting out of the same train that I had been on, all suffering from sciatica, as was clearly visible from the tremulous clenching of the buttocks, the halting gait and the somewhat helpless, pained facial expressions that accompanied every cautious movement. Each of them had his own speciality, his own variety of suffering, and hence his own way of walking, of hesitating, of hobbling, of limping, and each had his own form of grimace, but the predominant factor was what they had in common—I could see at a glance that all of them were sciatica sufferers, my colleagues, my brothers. Anyone who knows the games played by the *nervus sciaticus*—not by way of the medical handbook but from the personal experience which doctors call 'subjective sensation'—will understand exactly what I mean. I stopped in my tracks and gazed at these marked men. Lo and behold, all three or four were pulling faces worse than mine, were leaning more heavily on their sticks, flexing their hams more twitchily, treading more warily and fearfully—they were all more agonised, miserable, ailing and pitiful than me, and this did me a great deal of good, and remained a constantly recurring, inexhaustible source of comfort to me throughout my stay in Baden—everywhere you looked, there were people limping, people crawling, people sighing, people in wheelchairs, and they were far sicker than I was, and had far less reason for good humour and hope than I had! And so during the very first minute of my stay I had discovered one of the great secrets and magic potions of all health resorts, and I savoured my discovery with true delight—the Pain Cooperative Movement, the *socios habere malorum*.

When I left the platform and cheerfully tackled the gently sloping street that led down towards the baths in the valley, every step confirmed and enhanced this invaluable experience—patients were creeping and crawling everywhere, or sitting bent and weary on the green painted benches, or hobbling along in chattering groups. A woman was being pushed in a wheelchair, letting out a tired laugh, with a half-withered flower in her limp hand, while behind her, bursting with energy, strode her blossoming female carer. An elderly gentleman came out of one of the shops where rheumatics buy their postcards, ashtrays and paperweights (they need a lot of those, though I never found out why)—and this elderly gentleman who came out of the shop needed a minute to negotiate every step, and he looked at the road ahead of him like a man at the very end of his tether, suddenly confronted by a huge and unexpected task. A young man wearing a grey-green military cap on his bristly head was vigorously manipulating two sticks, though he could still scarcely move. Oh, those sticks, which were here, there and everywhere, those damnable, deadly serious sticks, which ended in rubber tips at the bottom and sucked on the asphalt like leeches or babes at the nipple! I too used a stick, a stylish malacca cane, whose support was most welcome, although if necessary I could also walk without it, but no one had ever seen me with one of those miserable rubber-tipped suckers. No, it must have been obvious to all who saw me how swiftly and athletically I sailed down this pleasant street, how infrequently but playfully I wielded my malacca cane—merely an ornament, a decorative accessory—how very slight and harmless was that characteristic sign of sciatica in me, the agonised clenching of the upper thigh, perhaps just hinted at, like the most rudimentary sketch, and how smoothly and elegantly I trod this path, how young and healthy I was compared with all these older, poorer, sicker brothers and sisters, whose afflictions revealed themselves so clearly, so undisguisedly, so relentlessly! From every step I drew their recognition, savoured their acknowledgement, and I felt almost fully fit, or at least infinitely less unfit than all these poor folk. Indeed, if these half-crippled hobblers could still hope to be cured, these rubber-tipped stick-walkers, if Baden could still help them, then my little beginner's pains must disappear like snow in the foehn, and in me the doctor would see a shining example, a phenomenon to give thanks for, a small miracle of curability.

Well, I enjoyed the pleasures of this first day to the very full, indulging in orgies of naive self-congratulation, and it was all highly beneficial. Drawn by the ubiquitous figures of my fellow patients, my less fortunate brothers, flattered by the sight of every cripple, inspired to joyful sympathy and empathetic self-satisfaction by every approaching wheelchair, I strolled down the street—that oh so cosily, comfortingly designed street, along which guests arriving from the station are wheeled to the baths, and which curves gently with a pleasant, even slope down to those ancient baths, thence to disappear like a dried-up riverbed into the entrances of the spa's hotels. Filled with good intentions and happy hopes, I approached the Heiligenhof, where I expected my journey to end. The idea was to spend three or four weeks here, taking the baths each day, walking as much as possible, and avoiding as much as possible all sources of anxiety and excitement. Perhaps it would occasionally become monotonous, and indeed it could hardly pass without periods of boredom, because the prescription here was the exact opposite of the high life, and for me—the old recluse deeply and painfully averse to any sort of domestic or hotel living—there would be a few problems to cope with, a few obstacles to overcome. But without a doubt this new, completely unfamiliar life, despite its perhaps rather bourgeois, rather soft-centred character, would bring me some interesting and entertaining experiences. And was it not high time that after years of living in primitive peace, in rural isolation, absorbed in my studies, I now spent some hours with my fellow humans again? And the main thing was that beyond the obstacles, beyond the now beginning weeks of treatment, lay the day on which I would make my sprightly way up this same pretty street, would leave behind these hotels and, healed and rejuvenated with elastically flexible knees and hips, would bid farewell to Baden as I danced my way to the station.

1923

A LESSON

Every word men speak, you may presume
Is more or less a fraud because, my dear,
You'll find us humans at our most sincere
Wrapped in our nappies, later in our tomb.

Then we are wise at last, and all is plain.
We join our fathers down below the ground
And with bare bones we rattle truth around
Though some would rather lie and live again.

THE FERRYMAN

WHEN HE REACHED THE ferry, the boat was ready and the same ferryman who had once taken the young *samana* across the river was standing in the boat; Siddhartha recognised him, though he too had aged considerably.

"Will you take me across?" he asked.

The ferryman, surprised to see such a distinguished gentleman wandering alone and on foot, helped him into the boat and cast off.

"You have chosen a fine life for yourself," said the passenger. "It must be nice living each day beside the water and travelling across it."

With a smile the oarsman rocked back and forth.

"It is fine, sir, it is indeed, as you say. But is not every life and every job nice?"

"That may be so. But I envy you yours."

"Oh, you would soon cease to enjoy it. It's nothing for people in fine clothing."

Siddhartha laughed. "I have already been noticed once today because of my clothes, and looked at with suspicion. Will you not, ferryman, take these clothes from me, as I am tired of them? For you should know that I have no money with which to pay the fare."

"The gentleman is joking," laughed the ferryman.

"I am not joking, my friend. Look, you have already taken me in your boat across the water once before, just for love. So do it again today, and take my clothes as payment."

"And does the gentleman intend to journey on without clothes?"

"Oh, I should like best not to journey on at all. I should like best, ferryman, for you to give me an old overall and to keep me on as your assistant, or rather as your apprentice, for first I must learn how to handle the boat."

For a long time the ferryman gazed enquiringly at the stranger.

"Now I know who you are," he said at last. "Once you slept in my hut, a long time ago, it may well be more than twenty years ago, and I took you across the river, and we parted as good friends. Were you not a *samana*? I can't remember your name now."

"My name is Siddhartha, and I was a *samana* when you last saw me."

"Then you are welcome, Siddhartha. My name is Vasudeva. You will, I hope, be my guest today as well and sleep in my hut, and tell me where you have come from and why you are so tired of your fine clothes."

They had reached the middle of the river, and Vasudeva pulled harder on the oars in order to make headway against the current. He worked in silence, his eyes fixed on the tip of the boat, his arms moving powerfully. Siddhartha sat and watched him, and recalled how long ago, on that last day of his time as a *samana*, love for this man had risen in his heart. Gratefully he accepted Vasudeva's invitation. When they reached the bank of the river, he helped him to tie the boat to the stakes, and then the ferryman invited him to enter his hut, offered him bread and water, and Siddhartha ate with pleasure, and with pleasure he also ate the mangoes which Vasudeva offered him.

Afterwards, they sat on a tree trunk on the bank— the sun was beginning to set—and Siddhartha told the ferryman where he came from and about his life, and how today, in his hour of despair, he had seen it all before his eyes. His tale went on deep into the night.

Vasudeva listened very attentively. He took it all in, origin and childhood, all the learning, all the seeking, all the joy, all the sorrow. This was one of the greatest of the ferryman's virtues—like few others, he knew how to listen. Without his saying anything at all, the speaker felt how Vasudeva absorbed his words, silently, openly, expectantly, not missing a single one, waiting without impatience, offering neither praise nor blame, but just listening. Siddhartha felt what happiness it was to confide in such a listener, to sink his own life, his own quest, his own suffering into the heart of another.

But towards the end of Siddhartha's tale, when he spoke about the tree by the river, and about his deep fall, about the holy Om and about how after his slumber he had felt such love for the river, the ferryman listened with redoubled attentiveness, completely and utterly engaged, his eyes tightly closed.

When Siddhartha fell silent, however, and there had been a long pause, Vasudeva said: "It is as I thought. The river has spoken to you. It is a friend to you and it also speaks you. That is good, that is very good. Stay with me, Siddhartha, my friend. Once I had a wife—her bed was next to mine, but she died long ago, and I have lived alone for a long time. Live with me now—there is room and food for both of us."

"I thank you," said Siddhartha, "I thank you and I accept. And I also thank you, Vasudeva, for listening to me so well! Rare are the people who know how to listen, and I have never met anyone who knew it as well as you. In this too I shall learn from you."

"You will learn it," said Vasudeva, "but not from me. The river taught me how to listen, and you too will learn from it. It knows everything, the river, and one can learn everything from it. You see, you have learnt that too from the river—that it is good to strive downwards, to sink, to search for the depths. The rich and noble Siddhartha will become an apprentice oars-man, the learned Brahman Siddhartha will become a ferryman—this too has been told to you by the river. You will also learn the other from it."

After a long pause, Siddhartha said: "What other, Vasudeva?"

Vasudeva stood up. "It is now late," he said. "Let us go to bed. I can't tell you about the 'other', my friend. You will learn it, and perhaps you already know it. You see, I am not a scholar, I don't know how to talk, and I don't know how to think. I only know how to listen and to be pious—otherwise I have learnt nothing. If I could say it and teach it, perhaps I should be a sage, but now I am just a ferry-man, and it is my task to row people across this river. Many have crossed it, thousands, and for all of them my river has been nothing but an obstacle on their travels. They travelled for money and on business, and to weddings and on pilgrimages, and the river was in their way, and the ferryman was there to help them overcome the obstacle as swiftly as possible. But some among the thousands, a few, four or five—for them the river ceased to be an obstacle; they heard its voice, they listened to it, and the river became sacred to them, as it is sacred to me. Now let us go and rest, Siddhartha."

Siddhartha stayed with the ferryman and learnt how to handle the boat, and when there was nothing to do on the ferry, he worked with Vasudeva in the rice field, collected wood and picked fruit from the pisang trees. He learnt to make an oar, to repair the boat, to weave baskets, and he was happy with everything he learnt, and the days and months raced by. But the river taught him more than Vasudeva could teach him. From the river he never ceased to learn. Above all, he learnt from it how to listen, to hearken with a silent heart, with a waiting, open soul, without passion, without desire, without judgement, without opinion.

He lived as a friend with Vasudeva, and sometimes they exchanged words—few but long-considered words. Vasudeva was not a friend of words, and Siddhartha seldom succeeded in getting him to speak.

"Have you," he once asked him, "have you also learnt this secret from the river—that there is no time?"

Vasudeva's face was covered with a bright smile.

"Yes, Siddhartha," he said. "Is this what you mean—that the river is everywhere at the same time, at its source and its mouth, at the waterfall, at the ferry, in the rapids, in the sea, in the mountains, everywhere, at the same time, and that for it there is only the present, not the shadow past, nor the shadow future?"

"That's it," said Siddhartha. "And when I had learnt it, I looked at my life and it too was a river, and the boy Siddhartha was separated from the man Siddhartha and from the old man Siddhartha only by shadows and by nothing real. And Siddhartha's earlier births were no past either, and his death and his return to Brahma will be no future. Nothing was, nothing will be; everything is, everything has being and presence."

Siddhartha spoke with delight, because this enlightenment had made him deeply happy. For was not all suffering time, was not all self-torment and self-terror time, were not all difficulties and all hostilities in the world overcome and gone as soon as one could think time away? He had spoken with delight, and Vasudeva smiled at him radiantly, nodded his affirmation, patted Siddhartha's shoulder with his hand, and returned once more to his work.

And on another occasion, when the river had swollen in the rainy season and was racing wildly, Siddhartha said: "Is it not true, my friend, that the river has many voices, very many voices? Does it not have the voice of a king and of a warrior and of a bull and of a night bird and of a woman giving birth and of a man sighing and a thousand other voices?"

"It is so," nodded Vasudeva, "all the voices of all creatures are in its voice."

"And do you know," continued Siddhartha, "what word it speaks when you succeed in hearing all its ten thousand voices at once?"

A happy laugh came from Vasudeva's face, and he leant against Siddhartha and whispered the sacred Om in his ear. And this was exactly what Siddhartha had also heard.

From time to time his smile was just like that of the ferryman, and was almost as radiant and almost as translucent with joy, similarly glowing from a thousand tiny folds, just as childlike, just as aged. Many travellers, when they saw the two ferrymen, thought they were brothers. In the evenings they often sat together on the tree trunk by the river, said nothing, and both listened to the water, which for them was not water but the voice of life, the voice of what is, of the endlessly becoming. And it sometimes happened that as they both listened to the river, they both thought of the same things, of a conversation two days ago, of one of their travellers whose face and fate concerned them, of death, of their childhood, and sometimes at the very same moment when the river had said something good to them, they would look at each other, both thinking exactly the same, both happy with the same answer to the same question.

The ferry and the two ferrymen radiated something that many of the travellers could sense. Sometimes it would happen that when a traveller had looked into the face of one of the ferrymen, he would begin to tell his life story, talk of his suffering, confess his sins, ask for comfort and advice. And sometimes it would happen that one would ask permission to spend an evening with them, in order to listen to the river. It also happened that curious people came who had been told that at the ferry lived two wise men, or sorcerers, or saints. The inquisitive ones asked many questions, but they were given no answers, and they found neither sorcerers nor sages, but just two friendly little old men, who seemed to be mute and a little strange and crazy. And the nosy ones laughed, and talked about how stupid and how credulous were the people who spread such rumours.

Extract from Siddhartha *1922*

For people with temperament, for artists, the decade between forty and fifty is always a critical time of unease and frequent dissatisfaction, in which one often has difficulty with life and with oneself. But then come years of calmness. I've not only experienced that within myself but have also observed it in many others. Lovely though youth may be, the time of fighting and ferment, maturing and growing old also has its beauty and its happiness.

From a letter written in
December 1955 to his son Bruno

HOW SWIFTLY THINGS PASS

I was a child but yesterday
Smooth of skin and loud with youthful laughter
And now I am an aged man already
Doing nothing till the end of day
With bloodshot eyes dimly gazing after
With bended back, walking on legs unsteady.
Oh how swiftly life just fades away.
Yesterday red, today blockhead
Tomorrow dead!
Had I not by my mistress been betrayed
And had my wife not from me run away
Then I'd go singing through the streets all day
And in the night lie snugly in my bed.
But when the women leave you high and dry
Give up, my son, because you cannot win.
Reach for the whisky, bear things with a grin
For now the time has come to say goodbye.

In the face of rights accepted by all humans, the
older man is in the wrong if he accepts the love of
a much younger woman and then lets her down,

because the older man should be the wiser and the more circumspect.

From a letter written c1925
to his wife Ruth

At the age of fifty a man gradually casts off certain childish things, the quest for reputation and respectability, and he begins to look back over his own life without passion. He learns to wait, he learns to stay silent, he learns to listen, and if these good gifts must be paid for with some illnesses and weaknesses, he considers that he has made a profit from the transaction.

Note written on the fiftieth birthday of
his wife Ninon 18th September 1945

THE MAN OF FIFTY

From the cradle to the bier
It will take but fifty year
Then death will claim his share.
You decline and you deteriorate
You despair and you disintegrate
And dammit you even lose your hair.
Your ancient teeth are moulding
And against your manly chest
There is no young lady pressed—
It's just a Goethe novel you are holding.

But one more time ere I depart
Let me embrace one of those girls
With sparkling eyes and tumbling curls
Whom I can hold against my heart
Kissing her lips, her face, her breast
And helping her to get undressed.
After that, in God's name then
Death can come for me. Amen.

One dies so damnably slowly, and piece by piece—
every tooth, muscle and bone says its own goodbye,
as if one had a special relationship with each of
them.

From an undated letter

We have to torment ourselves and eat many bitter
fruits before we lie still and rot ... A rocket has a
much better life—it goes whoosh, and is off at the
peak of its powers.

From a letter written on
25th April 1916 to Ernst Kreidolf

By youth we are forsaken
Our health too has declined.
The foreground now is taken
By the contemplative mind.

The older one gets and the less reason one actually has
for clinging to life, the more stupidly and fearfully one
shrinks away from death. And the more greedily and
childishly one falls upon the last crumbs of the meal,
the last few pleasures. And one keeps on hoping, and
one keeps on finding grounds for hope. Today, as the
fifty-year-old's fatal lust for life keeps me busy, I hope

for the time to come, for the stillness and detachment of the age that lies beyond these critical years.

From März in der Stadt
(March in the City), *1927*

I long for death, but not for a premature, immature death, and in all my yearning for maturity and wisdom I remain deeply and utterly in love with the sweet and capricious foolishness of life. We want both together, dear friend—lovely wisdom and sweet folly! We want to walk together and stumble together over and over again, for both should be delectable.

From a letter written on 20th
January 1917 to Walter Schädelin

I'm often surprised by the extreme toughness with which our nature clings to life. Compliantly, though by no means willingly, we adjust to circumstances which just two days ago would have seemed to us totally unbearable.

From a letter written in March
1956 to Peter Suhrkamp

Coming to terms with physical pain, when it lasts for some time, is certainly one of the hardest things to do. Those who are heroic by nature resist pain, try to deny it and grit their teeth like Roman Stoics, but admirable though this attitude might be, we still tend to have our doubts about whether pain can be truly conquered. As for me, I've always coped best with sharp pain when I have not resisted it, but have given myself over to it as one gives oneself over to inebriation or adventure.

From a letter written in
February 1930 to Georg Reinhart

Between fifty and eighty one can enjoy lots of nice experiences—almost as many as in the earlier decades. I would not recommend going past eighty, though—then it's not nice any more.

From a letter written in
April 1961 to Gunter Böhmer

64

ON GROWING OLD

Growing old is this: things you enjoyed
Are tiresome, muddy waters cloud the spring,
Of sharpness even pain is now devoid
For soon there'll be an end to everything.

And what we once regarded with resentment—
Commitment, duty, binding obligation—
Is now a source of refuge and contentment:
One more day's work would bring us consolation.

This bourgeois comfort too, though, cannot last—
The soul now longs to fly without a care.
It senses death, when time and self have passed
And deeply breathes it in like sweetest air.

REUNION WITH NINA

WHEN, AFTER MONTHS OF absence, I return to my hill in Ticino, I am always surprised and moved by its beauty—then it is not a matter of simply being back home, but first I must transplant myself, sink new roots, rebind old threads, return to old habits, and gradually rediscover feelings of past and home before my southern rural life begins to re-emerge. Not only do the suitcases have to be unpacked, and the country clothes and shoes located again, but I must also find out whether the winter rains have made their mark on the bedroom, whether the neighbours are still alive, and I must enquire what has changed here during my six-month absence, and what advances have been made in the process that is gradually robbing even this beloved place of its long-guarded innocence and is filling it with the blessings of civilisation. Indeed, down in the gorge below another slope has been deforested and a villa is under construction, and on a sharp bend our road has been widened, and an enchanting old garden has been made into an escape route. The last horse-drawn carriages have gone, and have been replaced by cars, but these new automobiles are much too big for our narrow lanes. And so I shall never again see old Piero in his blue postilion's uniform, with his yellow carriage and two bounding horses, racing down the hill, and I shall never again see him in the Grotto del Pace with his glass of wine, enjoying his little off-duty break. Alas, I shall never again sit at that beautiful forest's edge above Lugano, my favourite spot for painting—a stranger has bought both forest and field, and fenced it in with wire, and where there were once a few beautiful ash trees, now they're building a garage.

On the other hand, the grass below the vines is as green as ever, and from beneath the faded leaves scamper the same old blue-green emerald lizards, and the forest is blue and white with evergreens, anemones and strawberry blossoms, and shining up coolly and softly through this verdant forest is the lake …

Anyway, ahead of me lies a whole summer and autumn, and once again I'm hoping for a few good months, enjoying long days out in the open, being free for a while from my gout, playing with my paints, and living a happier, more innocent life than is possible in winter and in the cities. The years pass quickly—the barefooted children I saw going to school in the village when I first moved here are now married, or sitting at typewriters or behind counters in Lugano or Milan, and the elders of the village are dead and buried.

Now I remember Nina—is she still alive? Dear God, why have I not thought of her before? Nina is my friend, one of the few good friends I have in this region. She is seventy-eight years old, and lives in one of the most remote villages in the area, on which modern times have scarcely laid a finger. The path to her place is steep and difficult—I shall have to go down the hill for a few hundred metres in the baking sun, and then climb up again on the other side. But I set out at once, and first go downhill through the vineyards and forest, then across the narrow green valley, then steeply up the slopes which in summer are covered with cyclamen and in winter with Christmas roses. I ask the first child I meet in the village how old Nina is getting on. Oh, I'm told, she still spends her evenings sitting by the church wall taking snuff. Happily I go on my way—so she's still alive, I haven't lost her yet, and she'll give me a warm welcome, and even if she moans and groans a bit, she'll once more offer me the perfect model of a lonely old woman, stoically and not without humour enduring her gout and her isolation, standing no nonsense and making no concessions to the world, but spitting serenely in its face, and right to the end not bothering either doctor or priest.

I leave the dazzling road and go past the chapel in the shadows of the dark, age-old wall that winds its way defiantly along the rocky ridge and knows no time, no other present than the ever returning sun, no change but that of the seasons. Decade after decade, century after century. One day these old walls will also fall, and these lovely, dark and dirty quarters will be rebuilt with cement, metal, running water, hygiene, gramophones and other cultural artefacts, and over the bones of old Nina they will build a hotel with a French menu, or a Berliner will build himself a summer retreat. But today they are still standing, and I climb over the high stone threshold, mount the curved flight of stone steps and enter the kitchen of my friend Nina. As always it smells of stone and cold and soot and coffee and the intense odour of smoke from unseasoned wood, and on the stone floor in front of the huge fireplace, sitting on her low stool, is old Nina—she has lit a little fire in the fireplace, and the smoke is making her eyes water slightly, and with her brown, arthritic fingers she is pushing bits of wood back into the fire.

"Hello, Nina, do you recognise me?"

"Oh, *signor poeta, caro amico, son contento di rivederla!*"

She gets up, although I don't want her to—she stands up, which takes her a while, and then takes a few stiff-legged steps. In her trembling left hand she is holding the wooden snuffbox, and she has a black woollen shawl draped round her bust and back. Her sharp bright eyes gaze with a mixture of sadness and laughter from the beautiful old eagle face. She gazes at me with a teasing but affectionate expression. She knows *Steppenwolf*, and knows I am a *signor* and an artist, but that I'm not much good for anything and that I wander round Ticino all on my own, and have found as little happiness as she has, even though both of us have certainly kept an equally sharp lookout for it. What a pity, Nina, that you were born forty years too soon for me. What a pity. It's true that not everyone thinks you're beautiful, and some even think you're an old witch with those fiery eyes, those bent legs, those dirty fingers and that snuff in your nose. But what a nose it is in that wrinkled eagle face! What bearing, once she has pulled herself upright and stands at her full gaunt height! And how intelligent, how proud, how disdainful and yet not wicked is the expression in those finely carved, frank and fearless eyes! Old woman, what a beautiful girl you must have been, and what a beautiful, bold and spirited woman you must have become! Nina reminds me of past summers, of my friends, my sister, my mistress—all of whom she knows. In the meantime, she takes a quick look at the kettle, sees the water boiling, shakes some ground coffee out of the coffee grinder, makes me a cup, offers me some snuff, and then we sit by the fire, drink our coffee, spit into the flames, tell tales, ask questions, gradually fall silent, and say a few words about gout, winter and the uncertainty of life.

"Gout! It's a whore, a bloody whore! *Sporca puttana!* The Devil take it! I wish it would go to hell! Ah well, no use swearing. I'm glad you came, very glad. We should stay friends. Not many people come to see you when you're old. I'm seventy-eight now."

Once more she struggles to her feet and goes into the next room, where faded photographs are stuck in the mirror. I know she's now looking for a present to give me. She can't find anything, and so she offers me one of the old photographs as a gift, and when I refuse to take it, at least I have to have another sniff out of her snuffbox.

My friend's smoky kitchen is not very clean and is not at all hygienic—the floor is covered in spittle, the wicker from her chair hangs down in threads, and few of you readers would like to drink from her coffee pot, that old metal coffee pot which is black with smoke and grey with ashes, and whose sides are thickly crusted with dried-up coffee accumulated over the years. Life here is remote from the modern world and time, maybe pretty crude and grotty, pretty rundown, and anything but clean, but on the other hand it's close to the hills and forests, close to the goats and hens (they run clucking round the kitchen), close to witches and to fairy tales. The coffee from the battered old coffee pot smells wonderful—a strong, deep black coffee with a gentle aromatic hint of bitterness from the woodsmoke, and our sitting together drinking coffee, and the curses and the affection, and Nina's undaunted old face are infinitely more attractive to me than a dozen invitations to a tea dance, a dozen evenings of literary conversation in a circle of famous intellectuals, although of course I should not like to deny these charming occupations their relative value.

Outside, the sun is now setting, Nina's cat comes in and jumps onto her lap, and the light from the fire glows more warmly on the whitewashed stone walls. How cold, how cruelly cold winter must have been in this high and empty stone cave that contains nothing but the little open fire flickering in the fireplace, and the lonely old woman with gout eating her joints and no other company than the cat and her three chickens.

The cat is chased out. Nina gets up again and stands tall and ghostly in the twilight, a thin, bony figure with a shock of white hair falling over the sharply watchful eagle face. She won't let me leave yet. She invites me to be her guest for another hour, and goes to fetch bread and wine.

1927

AS WE GROW OLD

To be young and do good is a simple matter
On evil one's back to turn,
But to smile when the heart beats pitter-patter
Is something one has to learn.

And whoever succeeds has not grown old
But stands as bright as the sun
And has the world in his powerful hold
Bending its poles to one.

We think that death is waiting there
And so we should not stay
But march to meet him fair and square
And drive him far away.

But death's not here or there to see
Though everywhere displayed.
He is in you and is in me
When life we have betrayed.

Since old folk can't do anything else but give wise advice to young folk, I'll give you a few handy tips, because a man's sixtieth birthday is just the right time to do it. At this age it's time to give up some of one's youthful or manly pride and obstinacy, and start handling life—which one has hitherto bossed around—a bit more gently and warily. This includes a degree of care and attention and flexibility in relation to weaknesses and illnesses—one should stop moaning about them and forcing them to take a back seat, and instead one should give way to them and be nice to them, coddle oneself and, with doctors and medications, as with rest periods, taking the waters, having breaks at work, show them the respect they deserve, because they are all messengers from the greatest power that exists on earth.

From a letter written on
24th August 1947 to Max
Wassmer

FOR MAX WASSMER
ON HIS SIXTIETH BIRTHDAY

So far life hasn't been too bad
No one can say we didn't try—
Enough good laughs and drinks we've had
And felt the wild winds whistle by.
Some stupid things we've also done
Because we had our stubborn streak
That led to many a soulful sigh.
Life has pulled us to and fro
We've had our woes, we've had our fun.
I am ten years older, though,
And now I'm getting tired and weak.
But life's been full and life's been rich
With love, work, friends, all sorts of fests
With wine and music, laughing guests
And if life still can be a bitch
It's generally turned out fine
Thanks to the music and the wine
So all in all it's been a ball.
As time goes by, we may complain
That things no longer taste so sweet

And limbs and senses feel the strain
But we must bear our human fate.
Our minds go back to days of old
To memory's gardens bathed in light
Where beautifully preserved in gold
The flowers still blossom fresh and bright
And parties every day we hold.
And when, dear friend, you too grow tired
You'll find, like me, you're still inspired
By memories, for you'll have seen
How rich and royal life has been.
All is well, you've naught to rue
For you're a soul that's good and true
Who goes through life, bright and bold
Bringing joy to young and old
Wise and kind in all you do—
With radiant smiles we think of you.
Giver of pleasure, master of mirth
May you never have to part
From light of love and warmth of heart
Until your final day on earth.

The people who in their youth you can't possibly think of as old—they are the ones who make the best old folk.

From a book review

The most youthful of youngsters make the best old folk, and not those who behaved like grandfathers even when they were at school.

From Gertrud

The fact that young people like to show off a bit, and sometimes get away with doing daring things the old folk could never do themselves, is not so terrible when all is said and done. But it gets really bad at that miserable moment when the old, the weak, the conservative, the bald-headed, the die-hard old-fashioned take it personally and say to themselves: No question, they're only doing it to annoy me! From this moment on, it all becomes unbearable, and anyone who thinks like that is a lost soul.

From an undated letter

I've never felt attuned to youth being emphasised or organised; there's only young and old among hum-drum people; all gifted, differentiated people are old one minute and young the next, just as they're happy one minute and sad the next. Older people are able to act with more freedom, playfulness, experience, kind-heartedness in relation to their own capacity

79

for love than young people can. Age is quick to regard youth as precocious. But age itself always likes to imitate the gestures and movements of youth, is fanatical, is unjust, thinks it's always right and is easily offended. Age is not worse than youth; Lao Tse is not worse than Buddha. Blue is not worse than red. Age is only pathetic when it wants to play at being young.

From a letter written on
17th December 1930 to Wilhelm
Kunze

What has disgusted me for decades is firstly the idiotic worship of youth and all things young, such as is flourishing in America, and then even worse the establishment of youth as a status, a class, a 'movement'.

From a letter written on
9th December 1948 to Rolf Schott

I'm an old man and I like youth, but I'd have to tell a lie if I tried to say I'm really interested in it. For old people, especially in times as difficult as these, there is only one interesting question—that of the mind, of faith, of the kind of sense and devoutness that proves its own worth, that can cope with suffering and death. Coping with suffering and death is the task of age. Waxing enthusiastic, being with it, getting excited—that's the mood of youth. The one can talk to the other, but they speak two different languages.

From a letter written c1933
to Ernst Kappeler

The history of the world is basically created by the primitives and by the young, who take care of the onward movement and acceleration, in the sense of Nietzsche's somewhat theatrical aphorism: "What's going to fall should also be pushed." (Highly sensitive as he was, he could never have given such a push to an old sick person or animal.) However, if this history is to contain islands of peace and to remain bearable, it also needs delay and conservation as a counter-force, and this task falls to the old and cultured among us. But if the humans we think we are, and wish to be, were to follow different paths from our own, and evolve into beasts or ants, then it would indeed be our task to help slow this process as much as possible. Unconsciously, the militant forces in the world acknowledge the validity of this counter-movement in accordance with which—albeit pretty clumsily—they promote their cultural work alongside their weapons and their loudspeaker propaganda.

From a letter written on 12th–13th March 1960 to Herbert Schulz

SKETCH

Cold winds of autumn rustle through the withered reeds
Grey in the evening;
Crows flicker inland from the willow trees.

Standing still and alone on the strand, an old man
Feels the wind in his hair, the night and approaching snow.
He gazes across from the shadowed shore to the brightness
Where, between the clouds and lake, a band
Of distant shore still warmly glows in light—
The gold beyond, blissful as dreams and poems.

He holds the glowing image in his eye
And thinks of home, and thinks of his good years
Sees the gold grow pale, sees it die out
And then he turns away and very slowly
Wanders inland from the willow trees.

Growing old is not just a winding down and withering
—like every phase of life it has its own values, its own
magic, its own wisdom, its own grief, and in times of

a fairly flourishing culture, people have rightly shown age a certain respect, which nowadays is somewhat lacking in youth. We shall not hold that against youth. But we shall not let them talk us into thinking that age is worth nothing.

From a letter written on 10th January 1937 to Georg Reinhart

DYING

When children playing games I see
Their foolish laughter strange to me
And I no longer understand their play
I know it is a warning note
From an evil foe once so remote—
A foe from whom I cannot run away.

When I see young lovers kiss
And gladly leave them to their bliss
And Paradise has no appeal for me
Implicitly, alas, I part
With all the poetry of the heart
That promised to give youth eternity.

When I hear some vile oration
Don't react with indignation
Pretend I don't know what it's all about
Then I realise with a start
That there's a numbness in my heart
And the light that burned within is going out.

Growing old is in itself, of course, a natural process, and a man of sixty-five or seventy-five is, if he doesn't long to be younger, every bit as healthy and normal as one of thirty or fifty. But unfortunately people are not always on a level with their own age—inwardly they often rush ahead, and even more frequently they lag behind; then their conscious mind and feeling for life are less mature than their body, they resist its natural manifestations, and demand from themselves something that they cannot achieve.

From a letter written in 1935 to
Hans Sturzenegger

As one matures, one grows ever younger. That's how it is with me too, although that doesn't mean much because basically I've always maintained the same feeling for life that I had when I was a boy, and always felt that being grown up and getting old was some sort of comedy.

From a letter written on 24th January 1922 to Werner Schindler

Just as in youth, in times of beauty and enjoyment, one can never get enough of the pleasures of the eyes and the other senses etc, as one grows old it's the same with knowledge—one knows one must gather in as many as possible of the endlessly knowable things on earth, and that is a wonderful occupation.

From a letter written in 1938 to Fanny Schiler

[THE LAST JOURNEY
OF THIS KIND]

A Fragment

I ONCE KNEW A MAN who was nearly sixty years old and had led the life of an intellectual, and with such people it quite often happens that the body is neglected and becomes aged and decrepit long before the mind, and that's how it was with this man—although he had neither the burdens of office nor any great financial worries, and although he didn't lead the hectic life of the city-dweller but wasn't your actual stay-at-home either, age had prematurely marked and weakened him, and while his energy when in the service of his thoughts and work seemed just as great as ever, as soon as he had to make a physical effort or to exert his will in order to reach a decision, it would to a considerable degree desert him, and while the works of this intellectual were highly praised and had kept their youthful vigour, his physical everyday life had gradually become that of an old, sick man who suffered from all sorts of pains and problems, who had to be careful what he ate and drank, and in whose bedroom there were assembled more and more bottles, pots and glass tubes full of medicines. And so old age had crept up on him and caught him in its web, with the same slow and silent, almost imperceptible inevitability with which the apple ripens and the evening light fades away from the earth. Many people say that the natural processes of life occur in leaps, but I am more inclined to believe in the quiet, invisibly flowing forces of nature, as the poet Stifter describes them in the preface to his *Bunte Steine*. On the other hand, people frequently imagine they can see such leaps, both through perception and experience, when before their very eyes, after long slow preparation, something suddenly falls from the branch. That's how it is for most people when they grow old—it happens imperceptibly, but there are moments in which all at once a mirror is held up to the ageing man, he is confronted with a test, and then the hitherto unnoticed decline is abruptly, often shockingly revealed.

The man I'm talking about had travelled a lot when he was younger. Once a year he had gone to Italy and had spent days, or sometimes weeks wandering through stately old towns and villages, gazing up at towers and cathedrals, walking round collections of ancient works of art—an activity engaged in by so many since Winckelmann and Goethe, and for which his true model, whom he loved the most, was the scholar from Basel, Jacob Burckhardt. As well as Milan, Florence and Venice, in this manner he had got to know a large number of Italian towns, and many of them he liked so much that he often returned to them. Others, however, attractive and promising though they might have been, remained unvisited, and these were not so much the remote and inaccessible places as those very towns that lay on major railway routes and whose stations the man had frequently seen for himself, each time thinking that he should get out here too in order to change his book knowledge of these towns into living images and experiences, though each time also thinking that there was no hurry for him to do so.

The last journey of this kind was to Lake Garda, Lake Iseo and Brescia, and it had ended with a long and delightful trip on Lake Maggiore, from Arona to the northern end of the lake, on a day as clear as glass and with the foehn whipping the water, and as it later seemed to him, he had found it even more difficult than usual to bid farewell to Italy. This was in spring 1914, and it was to be his last journey to Italy, because shortly afterwards the Great War began, and when it was over the man had other things to think about than lovely, educational journeys—his youth and some of his *joie de vivre* had gone, and year followed year, difficult years and bearable years, and slowly, as the evening sun filters its light away until everything is grey, youth and the desire to travel and many other urges and many other lights filtered away and were lost from this man's life and feelings, until he stood on the spot where we first met him, in his sixtieth year, a diligent and intellectually still unwearied man, but a man with routines and with problems, with a lot of work and little leisure, still a long way from the end, still spared from any major illness, but fading all the same and barely mobile, no lover of parties, no lover of surprises and quick decisions, no longer the curious traveller and wanderer whose heart leaps at the sight of a distant blue mountain, a golden cloud hovering on the horizon, filling him with the joys of travel and an unquenched love for the beauty of the world.

Last year, he was badly affected by several personal blows and losses, and in suffering and enduring them he felt that they had struck at the very roots of his own life force. This bad period, however, was followed by a kinder one, in which he received signs of love and loyalty from old friends, so that gradually he regained his confidence and accustomed himself to accepting without defensiveness or irony this and that reference to the approach of his sixtieth birthday, and even secretly began to look forward to it. In this calm and indeed cheerful frame of mind, he also began to flirt with the idea of perhaps travelling once more to Italy, after a gap of over twenty years, and to try a trip to Tuscany or Umbria, wandering through beautiful foreign towns and landscapes, with all the little delights and adventures of a traveller's life. Of course he had long since given up making such journeys, even just for pleasure, and often enough he had expressed his dissatisfaction at the now fashionable forms of travel which, although they seemed to give people no less pleasure than in former times, still seemed to him unworthy of a person with taste. All these arrangements with travel agents, preoccupation with the current exchange rate, the superficial race through different countries whose languages and cultures the tourist didn't know, with Venice becoming just a village for an enjoyable evening on the beach, Marseille a restaurant for fish soup, Palestine and Egypt decorations for spoilt guests in luxury hotels—all of this seemed to him to be a sign of decadence and triviality, and if you objected that the world had grown younger, and instead of scholarly, meaningful journeys in the style of Goethe or Humboldt people nowadays quite rightly enjoyed simpler, more primitive and more easily digestible things like swimming pools and sport, and the carefree attractions for youth unsullied by intellect, then he would let out a scornful laugh and say that although he couldn't deny people were getting younger and younger, soon they would no longer need their swimming pools and sports facilities but, having got even younger, would be satisfied with the delights of thumb-sucking. Just lately, though, he seems to have forgotten these somewhat grumpy assertions—or at any rate, he hasn't let them stop him from once more thinking of travelling himself, and going to Italy …

c1936

NO REST

Bird of my soul, you never cease
One question fearfully to raise:
When, after all our riotous days,
Will there be rest, will there be peace?

I know we'll scarce have made our way
To silent stillness 'neath the ground
When there'll be yearnings newly found
To plague you every peaceful day.

And so you'll leave our resting place.
In search of suffering you'll go
And then impatiently you'll glow—
The newest star in space.

Whoever has grown old and is attentive can observe how, despite the decline of powers and potentials, with every year right to the very end a life goes on expanding and increasing the endless network of relationships and connections, and how so long as

memory remains alert, nothing of what passes and
is past is ever lost.

From Weihnachtsgaben
(Christmas Gifts) *1956*

DEAD LEAF

Each blossom to its fruit gives birth
Each morning dawns then leads to night
For nothing ever lasts on Earth
But all things change or else take flight.

Even the finest summer will
Feel autumn's chilly breath one day.
Be patient, leaf, and hold on still
Until the wind steals you away.

Play the game, there's no defence
So simply let it come
And let the wind just bear you hence
And blow you to your home.

[HARMONY OF MOVEMENT AND REST]

FOR MOST OLD PEOPLE, spring is not a good time—it also hit me hard. The powders and injections didn't help much; the pain spread as lavishly as the flowers in the grass, and the nights were tough going. Nevertheless, the few short hours each day when I was able to go outside brought me intervals of forgetting and dedication to the miracle of spring, and occasional moments of delight and revelation, every one of which would have been worth holding on to, if only there were a way of holding on, if only these miracles and revelations could be described and passed on. They take you by surprise, and can last for seconds or minutes, these experiences in which a process in the life of nature addresses us, displays itself to us, and if one is old enough, it seems as if one's whole life with joys and sorrows, with love and recognition, with friendships and love affairs, with books, music, travel and work has been nothing but a long diversion to the maturity of these moments, in which through the image of a landscape, a tree, a human face, a flower, God shows himself to us—the meaning and the value of all being and all happening is revealed to us. And the truth is, even if presumably in our younger years we have experienced more intensely and more dazzlingly the sight of a blossoming tree, a cloud formation, a thunderstorm, nevertheless for the experience that I'm referring to one does need great age, one needs the infinite sum of things seen, lived through, thought, felt and suffered, a certain frailty and proximity to death in order to perceive within a tiny revelation of nature the God, the spirit, the mystery, the coming together of opposites, the great oneness. Of course young people can experience this too, but less often, and without this unity of thought and feeling, of sensual and spiritual harmony, of stimulus and awareness.

During our dry spring, before the rains came with the sequence of stormy days, I often stopped at a place in my vineyard where at this time of year I build my campfire on a patch of still uncultivated soil. There, in the whitethorn hedge that closes off the garden, a beech tree has been growing for years—at first just a little shrub sprouting from a seed blown out of the forest; for several years I had somewhat reluctantly left it standing there just provisionally; I felt sorry for the whitethorn, but then the tough little evergreen beech flourished so prettily that eventually I accepted it, and now it's already a sturdy little tree and I love it twice as much because the mighty old beech, my favourite tree in all the nearby forest, was recently chopped down, and the pieces of its sawn-up trunk lie there with massive solidity like the stumps of ruined columns. My little tree is probably the child of that great giant.

It has always delighted and impressed me how persistently my little beech clings to its leaves. When everything else has long since been bare, it still stands there wrapped in the cloak of its dead leaves, all through December, January and February, and the wind pulls at it, snow falls over it and drops down from it, and those dry leaves, at first dark brown, become ever brighter, thinner, silkier, but the tree won't let them go, because they must protect the young buds. Then at some time every spring, each year later than expected, one day the tree has changed, has lost its old leaves, and replaced them with damply shining, tender new buds. This time I witnessed the change. It happened soon after the rain had left the countryside all green and fresh, one moment in the afternoon around mid-April, and so far this year I hadn't yet heard the cuckoo and had found no narcissi in the meadows. A few days earlier, I had stood here in a strong north wind, shivering, with my coat collar turned up, and I had watched with admiration as my beech tree stood there impassively in the biting wind and hardly yielding a leaf—tough and brave, stiff and stubborn, it held on to its bleached old foliage.

And now, today, as I stood in the gentle, windless warmth of my fire, breaking bits of wood, I saw it happen—there arose the softest of breezes, nothing but a breath, and in hundreds and thousands those leaves, so long preserved, came down, light and soundless, willingly, tired of their endurance, of their defiance and of their courage. What had held on for five or six months of dauntless resistance now, in a few minutes, gave in to a nothing, a mere puff, because the time had come, because the bitter struggle was no longer necessary. Down they floated and fluttered, smiling, ripe, without a fight. The little breeze was far too weak to carry the light, thin leaves very far, and so like fine rain they drizzled down and covered the path and grass at the foot of the tree, a few of whose buds had already opened and grown green. What had this astonishing and moving show revealed to me? Was it death, the easy and spontaneous death of the winter foliage? Was it life, the pushing, jubilant youth of the buds whose suddenly awakened will had created space for themselves? Was it sad, was it cheerful? Was it a warning to me, the old man, to let myself flutter and fall—an admonition that perhaps I too was taking up the space of those younger and stronger than myself? Or was it a command to hold on, like the leaves of the beech, and stay on my feet as long and as obstinately as I could, to brace myself and resist, because then, when the moment was right, the farewell would be easier and happier? No, like every such revelation, it was a manifestation of the great and the eternal, the coming together of opposites fused in the flames of reality; it meant nothing, and warned of nothing, or rather it meant everything, it meant the mystery of existence, and it was beauty, it was joy, it was meaning, it was a gift and a discovery for the onlooker, as Bach is for the ear and Cézanne for the eye. These names and meanings were not the experience itself—they only came later; the experience itself was just an appearance, a miracle, a mystery, as beautiful as it was serious, as sweet as it was inexorable.

At the same spot, by the whitethorn hedge and near the beech tree, now that the world had turned a juicy green and on Easter Sunday the first call of the cuckoo had graced our forest, one mild and changeable, windswept stormy day such as usually prepares the leap from spring to summer, the great mystery addressed me once more through a no less allegorical visual experience. In the heavily overcast sky, which nevertheless kept throwing bright sunbeams down into the budding green of the valley, the clouds were staging a great piece of theatre; the wind seemed to be blowing in all directions at the same time, though south-north seemed to be the favourite. The whole atmosphere was electric with the sound and fury. And in the midst of this spectacle, suddenly forcing itself into my view, stood another tree—a young and handsome tree, a freshly foliaged poplar in my neighbour's garden. It shot up like a rocket, waving, elastic, with pointed top, in the short intervals of windlessness closed up tight like a cypress, and as the wind strengthened gesticulating with a hundred slender, combed-out branches. The top of this lovely tree reared and rocked, its foliage gently flashing and whispering, rejoicing in its power and youthful greenness, softly swaying like the needle of a scale, at one moment giving way like a giant catapult, and then spontaneously springing back (not until much later did it occur to me that decades ago I had already been alert to this phenomenon, which I'd seen on a peach tree, and I had recorded it in the poem *Der Blütenzweig—The Flowering Branch*).

Joyfully, fearlessly and even mischievously, the poplar left its branches and leafy cloak to the mercy of the wet and swelling wind, and what it sang into the stormy day and what it wrote on the sky with its pointed top was beautiful, and perfect, and as light-hearted as it was serious, as much doing as being done by, as much fun as fate, and once again it contained all contrasts and contradictions. It was not the wind that was the winner and strong because it could shake and bend the tree; it was not the tree that was the winner and strong because each time it bent it could elastically and triumphantly spring back into position; it was the interplay between the two, the harmony of movement and rest, of heavenly and earthly powers; the endlessly elaborate dance of the treetop in the gale was only an image, only a revelation of the world's mystery, beyond strength and weakness, good and evil, done and being done by. For a little while, for a little eternity, in all this I could read the pure and perfect manifestation of what is otherwise concealed and secret, as if I were reading Anaxagoras or Lao Tse. And once again it seemed to me as if, in order to see this image and read this writing, I had needed not only the gift of an hour in spring, but also the deeds and misdeeds, the follies and lessons, the pleasures and pains of very many years and decades, and I felt the dear poplar tree which had presented me with this show to be nothing but a boy, innocent and inexperienced. It would have to be worn down by many frosts and snowfalls, shaken by many gales, slashed and scarred by many thunderbolts, until perhaps it too would be able to watch and listen and eagerly enquire into the great mystery.

From the circular letter
Aprilbrief (April Letter) *1952*

MARCH SUNSHINE

Drunk in the morning glare
A yellow butterfly flits.
By the window in his chair
A sleepy old man sits.

The spring was once a treat—
Singing without a care
He'd walked down many a street
Dust flying o'er his hair.

Although the blossoming bough
And golden butterfly
Seem no older now
Than in the years gone by

The aroma and the colour
Are not so sweet or bright.
The light is colder, duller
The air makes lungs feel tight.

HERMANN HESSE

Beneath the blue-white sky
The spring as softly sings
As humming bees. The butterfly
Spreads its golden wings.

ON AGE

OLD AGE IS A STAGE in our lives, and like all the other stages it has its own face, its own atmosphere and temperature, its own joys and needs. We old men with white hair, like all our younger human brethren, have the task of giving meaning to our existence, and even someone critically ill or dying, who lies in his bed scarcely able to hear a cry that comes from this world, still has his task—something to be done that is important and necessary. Being old is just as fine and sacred a task as being young; learning to die and dying is just as valuable a function as any other—provided it is done with respect for the meaningfulness and sanctity of all life. An old man who only hates his white hair and his proximity to death is as unworthy a representative of this phase of life as a young, strong man who hates his job and his daily work and tries to get out of them.

In brief, if an old man is to achieve his goal and do justice to his task, he must be in accord with age and with everything that age brings with it—he must say yes to all of it. Without this yes, without acceptance of what nature demands of us, we lose the value and the sense of all our days—whether we are old or young—and we betray life.

Everyone knows that old age brings its problems, and that death waits at the end of it. Year after year one must make more sacrifices and accept more deprivations. One must learn to distrust one's senses and one's powers. The path which not so long ago was just a little walk becomes long and tiring, and one day we can no longer manage it. We must give up the foods which all our lives we have so enjoyed eating. Physical joys and pleasures become rarer, and we must pay an ever greater price for them. And then all the breakages and illnesses, the weakening of the senses, the waning of the organs, the many aches and pains, especially in the long and fearful nights—none of this can be denied, for it is stark reality. But it would be sad and pathetic just to give in to this process of decay and not to see that old age has its good side, its advantages, its sources of comfort and enjoyment. When two old people meet, they should not speak only of their accursed gout, of their arthritic limbs and breathlessness on the stairs, they should not just exchange tales of their sufferings and annoyances, but they should also talk about cheerful and enjoyable experiences. And there are plenty of those.

When I refer to this good and positive side of an old man's life, and to the fact that we grey-haired folk are also acquainted with sources of strength and patience and pleasure that play no part in the lives of the young, I am not talking about the comforts of religion and the Church. That is the province of the priest. But I think I can gratefully give names to the gifts that are given to us by age. For me the dearest of all these gifts is the treasure of images which after a long life we carry in our memory, and to which with the decline of our active powers we turn with a different attitude from ever before. The figures and faces of people who left the earth sixty or seventy years ago still live on in us, are part of us, keep us company and look at us with eyes that are still alive. Houses, gardens, towns that have now disappeared or completely changed we can see unscathed, just as they were before, and distant mountains and coasts that we saw decades ago on our travels we rediscover fresh and colourful in our book of pictures. Looking, observing and contemplating increasingly becomes a habit, an exercise, and imperceptibly the mood and approach of the watcher permeates all our actions. We are haunted, like most people, by desires, dreams, yearnings and passions, under attack through the years and decades of our lives, impatient, tense, expectant, deeply affected by successes and failures— and today, gently leafing through the great picture book of our own life, we are amazed at how good and beautiful it can be to have escaped the hunt and the headlong rush and to have landed safely in the *vita contemplativa*.

Here, in this garden of old men, many flowers blossom which earlier we would never have thought of cultivating. There blooms the flower of patience, a noble plant, and we become calmer, more tolerant, and the less we insist on actively intervening, the greater becomes our ability to watch and listen to the life of nature and the lives of our fellow humans, and to let it all pass us by without criticism but with renewed amazement at the vast diversity, sometimes taking part or silently regretting, and sometimes laughing with shining joy and humour.

Recently I was standing in my garden, and had lit a fire which I fed with leaves and dry twigs. Then an old woman, probably about eighty, came walking past the whitethorn hedge, stopped and looked at me. I greeted her, and she laughed and said: "You're quite right to light a fire. At our age we need to gradually make friends with hell." With this she had set the tone of a conversation in which we moaned to each other about all kinds of sufferings and deprivations, but always making fun of ourselves. And at the end of our conversation, we confessed to each other that in spite of everything, we were not at all so dreadfully old and indeed could hardly call ourselves old so long as the oldest inhabitant of our village, a centenarian, was still alive.

When the very young, with their superior strength and their innocence, laugh at us behind our backs and mock our hobbling gait, our few white hairs and our scraggy necks, then we remember that once we had the same strength and innocence and also smiled, and we do not see ourselves as inferior or vanquished, but rejoice that we have grown out of this phase of life and have now become just a little wiser and a little more patient.

1952

AUTUMN RAIN

O rain, you autumn rain
And hills all veiled in grey
Trees weighed down with weary foliage!
It's hard for the ailing year to leave
Gazing through the steamed-up windows.
Shivering in your dripping coat
You stand outside. And at the forest's edge
There stagger from the bleached leaves
Drunken toads and salamanders.
Along the paths that run downhill
Endless waters stream and gurgle
Till they reach the grass and fig tree
Where they stand in patient pools.
And from the church tower in the valley
Tired and timid comes the sound
Of tolling bells for some dead villager
Being buried in the ground.

But you, dear friend, should not be grieving
For the neighbour being buried
Nor for summer's pleasures passing
Nor for festive joys of youth!
All things are kept in pious memory
Preserved in word, picture and song
Ever ready to return in splendour
Dressed in newer and in finer robes.
Help to preserve, help to change
And the flower of faithful joy
Will blossom in your heart.

Age has many hardships—but it also has its gifts of grace, and one of them is the protective layer of forgetting, of weariness, of submission which allows things to grow between us and our problems and sufferings. There may be inertia, calcification, hideous apathy, but there can also be—illuminated a little differently by the moment—serenity, patience, humour, deep wisdom and Tao.

From Rigi-Tagebuch
(Rigi Diary) *1945*

Old age helps you overcome many things, and if an old man shakes his head or murmurs a few words, then some see worldly wisdom in them, others merely ossification; whether his approach to the world is basically the result of experience and wisdom or simply the consequence of circulation problems remains undiagnosed, even by the old man himself.

From a letter written in November
1942 to Lajser Ajchenrand

Only when you grow old do you see the rarity of beauty, and what a wonder it really is when flowers bloom between factories and cannons, and poetry still lives between newspapers and stock-market reports.

From a letter written in November
1930 to Hans Carossa

For them, the young, their own existence, their searching and suffering, quite rightly is of prime importance. For the man who has grown old, the search was a false trail, and life has gone wrong if he has found nothing objective, nothing above himself and his cares, nothing absolute or divine to worship, in the service of which he can place himself, and the service of which alone can give his life meaning …

117

The necessity for youth is to be able to take itself seriously. The necessity for age is to be able to sacrifice itself, because above it is something that does take things seriously. I don't like formulating doctrines, but I truly believe that a spiritual life must run and play between these two poles. For the task, desire and duty of youth is to become, and the task of the mature man is to surrender himself or, as German mystics used to call it, 'to de-become'. One must first be a full person, a real personality, and one must have undergone the sufferings of this individualisation before one can make the sacrifice of this personality.

From a letter written in
January 1933 to M K

A GREY WINTER'S DAY

It happens one grey winter's day.
All's still, the light is dim
A grumpy old man makes his way—
No one should speak to him.

He hears the flood of youth go by
Full of storm and stress
Profane and pointless to his eye
This rash almightiness.

Mockingly he knits his brow
The grey light fades apace
The snow is gently falling now
He covers up his face.

Up in the bare-branched mountain ash
Troubling his old man's dreams
Squabbling blackbirds, loud and brash.
He hates the seagulls' screams.

Silently he'll scorn and scold
Such pompous proud display.
And so into the dark and cold
He wends his hoary way.

It should not be important to us to keep or copy the past, but we should be adaptable enough to experience the new and to engage ourselves in it with all our strength. In this context, grief in the sense of holding on to what has been lost is not a good thing, and is not in accord with true life.

From a letter written on
28th July 1916 to his sister Adele

A SMALL BOY

When they punish me
Very quiet I keep.
I cry myself to sleep
And waking up I'm free.

When they punish me
I refuse to weep.
A small boy's all they see
But I laugh in my sleep.

Grown-ups finish dead—
Gramps and Uncle passed away—
But I shall live instead
For ever and a day.

My life—this is what I decided—should be a transcendence, an advance from one stage to another; it should be a space around which others tread and then are left behind, just as music moves theme by theme, tempo by tempo, played, finished and left behind, never tired, never sleeping, always awake, always completely present. In connection with experiences of awakening, I had realised that such stages and spaces exist, and that the last phase of every section of life has within it overtones of decline and of a death wish, which then leads to a movement into another space, another awakening, a new beginning.

From Das Glasperlenspiel
(The Glass Bead Game) *1943*

STAGES

Just as youth has to give way to age
And flowers must fade, so at every stage
All things of virtue, beautiful and clever
Must bloom and fade, for naught goes on for ever.

With each fresh call from life, prepare the heart
To say goodbye, and then once more to start.
Be bold and brave, for there is nothing tragic
When bright new opportunities arrive
Since all beginnings hold a kind of magic
That shields and helps us all to be alive.

From room to room let's go, to none retire
For gladly we should leave each one behind us.
The World Spirit does not wish to bind us
But step by step to raise us ever higher.

Scarcely have we made a place our home
When familiarity begins to weigh.
Only those who are prepared to roam
From chains of deadening habit break away.

Perhaps one day even the final knell
Will have yet more new rooms for us in store
And life will go on calling evermore ...
And so, my heart, take leave and fare you well!

Against the infamies of life, the best weapons are these: boldness, obstinacy and patience. Boldness strengthens, obstinacy is fun, and patience keeps you calm. Unfortunately, one usually acquires these only late in life, and it is as one withers and fades away that one has most need of them.

From a letter written on
23rd July 1950 to H S

Nostalgia for a lost home is very similar to grieving over one's childhood and one's childish beliefs. We should not nourish or nurture such longings or make ourselves ill with them, but we should apply these spiritual powers to the present and to reality.

A very large proportion of the human race today is homeless, and by adapting themselves to new places, people and tasks, these folk must try to make a home in the unknown.

From a letter written in February 1960 to a young person

In the midst of overwhelming machinery, we must recapture nature, and after an exhausting day's work make it possible to stop, and to get to the middle of the centrifuge. Forces that may help to achieve this are nature, music and above all one's own creative powers.

From a letter written in December 1958 to a reader

Next to the gifts of the mind and of art, those of nature are the only ones that never leave us in the lurch when things get really serious.

From a letter probably written in the 1940s to Erna Klärner

LANGUAGE OF SPRING

Every child knows the language of spring—
Live and grow, bloom and hope, be true
Love, and always find new things to do.
Enjoy your life, and don't fear anything!

Every old man knows the language of spring—
It's time, so let them put you in the earth
Let the boys take your place with mirth
And so give way, for death's no fearful thing!

For old people generally, spring is not a pleasant time. Just as the foehn shakes and tests every old tree branch by branch, to see if it can't break it down, so the spring shakes old people to see if soon they'll be rotten enough. All the same, it's beautiful.

> *From a letter written at Easter 1948*
> *to Karl Kloter*

To grow old in a humanly dignified manner and yet at all times to maintain the attitude and wisdom appropriate to our age is a difficult art; generally our soul is either ahead of our body or behind it, and among the correctives to these discrepancies are those shocks to our inner feelings of life, those tremblings and fears at the very roots which again and again befall us through episodes of our lives or through illness. It seems to me that one should both be and feel small when confronted by them, just as a child can best restore its balance after some disturbance in life through weakness and weeping.

From a letter written on 22nd May
1935 to Joseph Feinhals

As far as the wisdom of age versus the passions is concerned, indeed it is a good thing, but age—since it is also a part of life—continually brings us into new situations, in relation to which we are not wise because they are new and require new thoughts. And so one goes on making experiments and doing silly things, and the only advantage one has over the young is a plus for patience.

From a letter written c1943 to Else Marti

When one reaches a great age, one looks back at the remarkable sights of a long past life. The second half of my life was the dramatic one, rich in battles, rich in enemies, in bad times and finally in all too much success. But the power to survive this unruly second half came from the first, calmer half, from the almost forty years of peace that I was lucky enough to experience. People have spoken of the War as a baptism of fire. But in my experience it is only peace that advances people and gives them strength.

From a circular letter written in August 1958

What would things be like for us old people if we didn't have this—the picture book of memory, the treasure of our experiences! It would be lamentably miserable. But in this we are rich, and we carry not only our worn-out body towards the end and oblivion, but also that treasure which lives and lights so long as we can breathe.

From an undated letter

WEARY EVENING

Evening winds mumble
With groans the trees resound
Heavy raindrops tumble
Singly to the ground.

From cracks in crumbling walls
Ferns and mosses sprout
And old folk from their halls
Silently peep out.

On bony stiff knees pressed
Crooked fingers lie
And all prepare to rest
And then to fade and die.

Over the graveyard wheels
A large and heavy crow
And on the flat-topped hills
Ferns and mosses grow.

We and wisdom are like Achilles and the tortoise. It is always a little way ahead of us. But to be on our way to it, and to follow its powers of attraction, is a good path to take.

From a letter written c1950 to
Hans Huber

Wonderful magic, glowingly sad magic of the ephemeral! And even more wonderful, the not-being-past, the not-being-extinguished-ness of what has been, its mysterious survival, its mysterious endlessness, its wakability in the memory, its being buried alive in the ever retrievable word!

Diary entry 14th May 1953

THE OLD MAN AND HIS HANDS

Until the long, long night is over
His weary way he makes
And watches when he wakes
And there at rest upon the cover
Sees his hands, both left and right
Worn-out servants, wooden, tight
And he chuckles
Softly, not to wake his knuckles.

Undaunted, they've worked hard and true
When most have had enough
For they're still strong and tough.
There's even more that they could do.
But though these faithful vassals stay
They'd like to rest and turn to clay
And say goodbye
To serfdom, for they're drained and dry.

Softly, not to wake his fingers
The old man laughs again
And life's long winding lane
Seems short, and yet the night still lingers
On and on … And children's hands
And young men's hands, and old men's hands
Look just like these when all the sands
Of time have gone.

THE LITTLE CHIMNEY SWEEP

ON SHROVE TUESDAY AFTERNOON my wife had to go to Lugano at very short notice. She tried to persuade me to accompany her, as we could then spend a little time watching people wandering around in their carnival costumes, or we might even watch a parade. I wasn't exactly in the mood, having been suffering for weeks from pains in all my joints, and in my state of semi-paralysis I jibbed at the very thought of having to put on my coat and get into the car. But after a certain amount of resistance, I finally plucked up some courage and agreed to go. We went down to the landing stage, where my wife dropped me before she drove off to find a parking place, and I waited with Kato, our cook, in watery but still perceptible sunshine in the midst of a gently bustling flood of activity. Even on an ordinary day, Lugano is an extremely cheerful, friendly town, but today every alleyway and every square was laughing at its merriest and most boisterous—the colourful costumes were laughing, the faces were laughing, the windows of the houses

135

on the piazza were overflowing with laughing masks and laughing people, and today even the noise of the town was laughing. It consisted of shouting, waves of laughter and people calling to one another, snatches of music, the funny, echoing boom of a loudspeaker, screeches and screams of mock terror from girls being bombarded by boys with fistfuls of confetti, the obvious main purpose being to try and stuff a load of it into the mouth of the victim. The streets were all covered with these multicoloured scraps, and under the arches you felt as if you were walking on a soft carpet of sand or moss.

My wife soon returned, and we took up our positions in a corner of the Piazza Riforma. This square seemed to be right at the heart of the festival. The square and the pavements were crowded with people, but in between the bright and noisy groups of standing spectators there was also a continuous coming and going of strolling couples or members of different societies, including lots of children in fancy dress. On the far side of the square a stage had been erected, on which several people performed their lively acts in front of a loudspeaker: an MC, a folk singer with guitar, a vulgar clown and various others. You listened or you didn't, you understood or you didn't, but you laughed anyway when the clown hit a familiar nail on its familiar head, actors and audience interacted, with those on- and offstage goading each other on, and there was a continual exchange of goodwill, sparks flying, fun and games and everyone ready to laugh. The MC introduced a youth to his fellow citizens—a young and very gifted amateur artiste, who delighted us with his virtuoso imitations of animal calls and other sounds.

I'd promised myself that we would only stay for a quarter-of-an-hour at most in the town. However, we stayed for a good half-hour happily watching and listening. For me, stopping in a town in the midst of a crowd—even in a festive town—is highly unusual and half frightening, half intoxicating. I live for weeks and months on end in my studio and my garden, and very rarely rouse myself enough to go as far as the village or even the end of our own plot of land. Now, suddenly, there I was surrounded by crowds of people, in the middle of a laughing, joking town, laughing with them, and enjoying the sight of human faces, so many types, full of changes and surprises, once more one among many, part of the whole, and swimming with the tide. Of course it wouldn't last for long, and soon my cold aching feet and my tired aching legs would have had enough and would long to go home, and soon too the charming little episode of intoxicating sights and sounds, the vision of these thousand so wonderful, so beautiful, so interesting, so lovable faces, and the hearing of these many voices, these speaking, laughing, screaming, giggling, ordinary, high, deep, warm or harsh human voices would have exhausted me; my cheerful surrender to the rich abundance of visual and aural pleasures would be followed by fatigue and a fear, bordering on vertigo, of this welter of no longer controllable impressions. "I know, I know," Thomas Mann would say now, quoting Effi Briest's father. If one took the trouble to think about it for a moment, it wasn't just the weaknesses of old age that were to blame for this fear of excess, of the world's abundance, of the dazzling illusions of Maya. Nor, to use the terms of the psychologist, was it simply the introvert's fear of having to prove himself to the world around him. There were other, to a certain degree better reasons for this gentle, vertigo-like fear and susceptibility to weariness. When I saw my neighbours, who throughout that same half-hour had been standing near me in the Piazza Riforma, it seemed to me that they were like fish in water, at ease, tired but happy, under no sort of pressure; it seemed to me that their eyes took in the images, their ears the sounds, as if behind the eyes there was not a film, not a brain, not a store and an archive, and behind the ears there was not a record or a tape, at every second busy collecting, gathering, recording, duty-bound not only to enjoy but also—and far more importantly—to preserve in order later perhaps to replay, obliged to register everything with the greatest possible degree of precision. In brief, once more I was standing there not as a member of the audience, not as a witness and a listener without responsibility, but as a painter with sketchbook in hand, working, straining every sinew. Because this was our way, the artist's way, of enjoying and celebrating—it consisted in working, in obligation, and yet all the same it was pleasure, so long as there was still enough strength, so long as the eyes could bear the constant toing and froing between scene and sketchbook, so long as the archive in the brain still had space and the ability to expand. I would never be able to explain this to my neighbours if they were to ask me or if I wished to make the effort myself; they would probably laugh and say:

"*Caro uomo*, stop moaning about your job! It's just a matter of watching and eventually describing funny things, which may seem demanding and hard work to you, whereas as far as you're concerned the rest of us are enjoying our holiday, gawping and lazing around doing nothing. But we really are on holiday, neighbour, and we're here to enjoy ourselves, not to do our jobs like you. Only our jobs are not as nice as yours, signore, and if you had to spend a single day like us in our shops or workshops, factories or offices, you'd soon be shattered."

He's right, my neighbour, absolutely right—but it doesn't help, because I think I'm right too. But we tell each other our truths without any resentment on either side—amicably, and with a bit of a twinkle in the eye, each of us wishing only to justify himself a little, but not wishing to hurt the other's feelings.

All the same, the arrival of such thoughts, or simply imagining such conversations and justifications, was enough to set off feelings of renunciation and fatigue—it would soon be time to go home and catch up on the midday rest that I'd missed out on. And alas, how few of the fine images of this half-hour had made their way into the archive to be saved! How many hundreds, maybe of the finest, had passed by my indolent eyes and ears leaving as little trace as in those people I thought myself justified in calling gawpers and holiday-makers!

One of the thousand images, however, did remain, and is to be recorded for friends in my little sketchbook.

Standing near me for almost the whole of my stay in the festive piazza was a very still and silent figure;

I didn't hear him say a word throughout the half-hour, and I scarcely saw him move—he just stood there in strange isolation, or reverie, in the midst of the colourful hustle and bustle, as still as a painting and very beautiful. He was a little boy, seven years old at the most, a pretty little fellow with the inno-cent face of a child—for me the most lovable face of all the hundreds. He was wearing a costume—a black robe, a black top hat, and one arm was thrust through a little ladder; there was a chimney sweep's brush too, and all of this was carefully and beauti-fully made, while the dear little face was coloured with a bit of soot or some other black stuff. But he wasn't aware of any of this. Unlike all the other grown-up Pierrots, Chinese, pirates, Mexicans and Biedermeiers, and in total contrast to the performers on the stage he had no consciousness at all of the fact that he was wearing a costume and represented a chimney sweep, or of the fact that this was some-thing special and funny and suited him so well. No, he just stood there, small and still, in his place, his tiny feet in his tiny brown shoes, his black polished ladder over his shoulder, hemmed in by the crowd and occasionally jostled without even noticing it, with his dreamily enchanted, bright blue eyes staring from his smooth-skinned child's face with blackened

141

cheeks up at a window in the house before which we were standing. There in the window, a man's height above our heads, was a jolly collection of children, a bit bigger than him, laughing, shrieking and pushing each other—all of them in bright fancy dress, and from time to time showering us with handfuls or bagfuls of confetti. With a kind of reverent rapture, lost in blissful admiration, the little boy's eyes gazed upwards, astonished, fascinated, inexhaustibly and magnetically drawn to the sight. There was no longing in his expression, no burning desire, but just total absorption and grateful delight. I couldn't make out what it was that so amazed this young soul, filling him with the unique joy of watching and being enraptured. It might have been the resplendent colours of the costumes, or a first realisation of the beauty of girls' faces, or the attentiveness of a lonely child who had no brothers or sisters, listening to the social chatter of the pretty children up above—or perhaps the boy's eyes were simply bewitched by the magic of the gently drifting shower of colours sinking down every so often from the hands of his idols, collecting in thin layers on the heads and clothes, and more densely on the stone slabs below, which were already covered as if in fine sand.

And my feelings were like those of the boy. Just as he perceived nothing about himself and the attributes and intentions of his disguise, nothing of the crowd, the clowns on stage and the laughter and applause that rippled through the spectators in throbbing waves, but kept his eyes fixed immovably on the window, so too were my eyes and heart, in the midst of all these urgently competing images, fixed on and devoted to only one image—the child's face between the black hat and the black robe, his innocence, his sensitivity to beauty, his unselfconscious happiness.

1953

THINKING BACK

The hills are purple with heathery sheen.
The branches of the brown broom sway.
But who knows now how rich and green
The forest was in May?

Who knows now how blackbirds sang
And who can hear the cuckoo's call?
The sounds that once so sweetly rang
Are lost beyond recall.

Above the hills a full round moon
Midsummer parties in the wood—
Who captured them, who wrote them down?
Now they're gone for good.

Soon you and I will disappear
Unknown, we'll be on no one's list.
Others will be living here
And we shall not be missed.

We'll wait for the evening star in the sky
And the morning mist across the sward
And we'll gladly blossom, gladly die
In the garden of the Lord.

[CHANGING BACK]

I T IS PART OF the mood and strange lack of consistency in one's later years that life loses a lot of its reality, or of its proximity to reality, and that reality, which itself is already a somewhat insecure dimension of life, becomes thinner and more translucent, its claims on us no longer make their presence felt with the same force and relentlessness of earlier times, and it allows us to talk to it, play with it and handle it. Reality for us old people is no longer life but death, and we no longer wait for it as for something external, but we know that it dwells within us; although we resist the pains and problems that its proximity inflicts on us, we do not resist death itself—we have accepted it, and if we care for and coddle ourselves rather more than we did before, we care for and coddle death too, because it is with us and in us, and is our air, our task, our reality.

What's more, the world and the realities that were once all around us lose much of their truthfulness and even their probability, for they are no longer obviously and indisputably valid, and we can take

147

them or leave them—we have a certain power over them. Thus everyday life takes on a kind of playful surrealism, because the old fixed systems are not quite so authoritative, aspects and emphases have shifted, the past increases in value compared to the present, and the future is of no serious interest whatever to us. And so our day-to-day conduct, from the standpoint of reason and the old rules, becomes somewhat irresponsible, frivolous, playful—the sort of behaviour that is popularly known as 'being childish'. There is a lot of truth in that, and I have no doubt that I often innocently and irresistibly react in childish ways to the world around me. But observation teaches me that these reactions are definitely not always so innocent or uncontrolled. Old people can do childish, impractical, unprofitable and playful things with total (or semi-) consciousness, and with the same sort of pleasure as a child feels when it talks to a doll or according to its own mood and imagination magically transforms its mother's little kitchen garden into a jungle full of tigers, snakes or hostile Indian tribes.

Here's an example—it was the hour when after reading the morning post I would go out into the garden. I say 'garden', although in fact it's a pretty steep, very overgrown grassy slope with a few vine-covered terraces that are well cared for by our good old hired hand, while the rest shows a pronounced tendency to change back into virgin forest. Where two years ago we still had a meadow, the grass is now thin and bare, and instead there are flourishing anemones, Solomon's seal, Paris quadrifolia, bilberries, here and there even a few blackberries and heather, and a lot of woolly moss all over the place. The moss and all its neighbouring plants would have to be grazed by sheep, and the ground trampled on by their hooves, if the meadow was to be saved, but we haven't got any sheep, we wouldn't have any manure to fertilise the rescued field, and so year by year the tough roots of the bilberries and their comrades creep deeper and deeper into the grassland, and the earth thus reverts to being a forest floor.

According to whatever mood I'm in, I see this transformation either with ill humour or with good grace. Sometimes I have a go at a piece of this dying meadow, attack the rampant wild plant life with rake and fingers, mercilessly comb out the mossy upholstery between the endangered bunches of grass, rip out a basketful of bilberry tendrils complete with roots, without believing for one moment that this will do the slightest bit of good, as my gardening in the course of the years has become nothing but a hermit's pastime without any practical meaning—that is to say,

it has a meaning for me alone, which is a matter of
personal hygiene and economics. When the pains in
my eyes and head become too much for me, I need
to change over to some mechanical activity, a physical
occupation. The horticultural and charcoal-burning
make-believe work that I have devised over the long
years not only serves the purpose of this physical
change and relaxation, but it also helps me to medi-
tate, to continue spinning threads of fantasy and to
concentrate on matters of the soul. And so from time
to time I try to make it a bit more difficult for my
meadow to turn into forest. At other times, I stop in
front of the wall we built up more than twenty years
ago on the southern edge of the property—it's made
of earth and the countless stones we dug up when we
were making a trench to hold back the neighbouring
forest, and once we planted it with raspberry canes.
Now this wall is covered with moss, grass, ferns and
bilberries, and a few already quite imposing trees,
including a shady lime tree, stand as the advance
guard of a slowly encroaching forest. On this particular morning, I had no objections to the moss or the
undergrowth, or the overgrowth or the forest itself,
but I gazed on the world of wild plants with pleasure
and admiration. And all over the meadow there were
lots of young narcissi, with fleshy leaves, not quite

blooming, their calyxes still closed, not yet white but a gentle yellow, the colour of freesias.

Anyway, I walked slowly through the garden, looked at the young, reddish-brown rosebushes through which the morning sun was shining, and the bare stems of the newly bedded-out dahlias between which with boundless vitality soared the thick stalks of the Turk's cap lilies, heard our faithful vine man Lorenzo clattering around further down with his watering cans, and decided to have a chat with him and discuss all sorts of gardening politics. Slowly I went down the slope, terrace by terrace, armed with an implement or two, enjoyed looking at the grape hyacinths in the grass, which many years ago I had scattered in hundreds all over the slope, wondered which bed would be best this year for the zinnias, was delighted to see the wallflowers in bloom, and dismayed to see the gaps and crumbling areas in the fence of latticed branches we'd put round the top compost heap, which was covered in the beautiful red of the fallen camellia blossoms. I climbed all the way down to the level vegetable garden, said hello to Lorenzo, and started off the conversation I'd planned by asking how he and his wife were, and exchanging views on the weather. I thought it was a good thing that there was evidently some rain on the way. Lorenzo, however, who is almost as old as I am, leant on his spade, threw a quick glance up and across at the driving clouds, and shook his grey head. There wouldn't be any rain today. You never know, surprises can happen, although … and once more he squinted knowingly skywards, shook his head vigorously and ended the rain discussion: "No, signore."

Next we talked about vegetables, including the freshly planted onions, and I was full of praise for everything as I guided the conversation round to what I was really after. The fencing round the top compost heap probably wouldn't last much longer, and I'd advise rebuilding it, although of course not now, when he already had his hands full with so many other things to do, but maybe some time getting towards autumn, or winter even? He agreed, and we decided that when he did get round to this job, it would be best not to renew just the lattice of green chestnut branches but also the posts. Although they might stand up for another year or so, it would be advisable … Yes, I said, and while we were on the subject of the compost heap, I'd also be grateful if in autumn he wouldn't put all the really good soil on the higher beds again, but would set some aside for my flower terrace—at least a few wheelbarrowfuls. Right? And we shouldn't forget to increase the strawberries this year, and clear out the lowest strawberry bed down by the hedge, which had been there all these years. And so each of us in turn came up with good and useful ideas for the summer, for September, for the autumn. And after we'd discussed everything, I carried on, while Lorenzo went back to work, and both of us were pleased with the outcome of our conversation.

It had not occurred to either of us to tackle one awkward subject that was perfectly familiar to both of us and would have ruined the conversation and rendered all our decisions illusory. We had negotiated with each other straightforwardly and in good faith—indeed with too much good faith. And yet Lorenzo knew just as well as I did that this conversation, with all its plans and good intentions, would not remain in his memory or in mine, and within a fortnight at most we would both have forgotten every single word months before the times set for the rebuilding of the compost heap and the expansion of the strawberry beds. Our morning chat beneath a non-rainy sky had taken place purely for the sake of talking—a game, a divertimento, a totally aesthetic activity that would have absolutely no consequences. It had been sheer pleasure for me to gaze for a while into Lorenzo's dear old face and to be the recipient of his diplomacy, which established a protective wall of the most delicate courtesy between himself and his interlocutor, without ever taking the latter seriously. As contemporaries, we also have a feeling of fraternity towards one another, and when one of us is limping particularly badly, or is having extra difficulties with his swollen fingers, although we don't actually talk about it, the other will smile understandingly with a slight feeling of superiority, and on this occasion will experience a certain satisfaction based on a sense of solidarity and sympathy in which he is not displeased at being temporarily the more robust of the two but, at the same time, is made to think with anticipatory regret of the day when the other will no longer be standing there beside him.

From Notizblätter um Ostern
(Notes at Easter) *1954*

MAXIM

To all things you should be
Brother or sister true
So they merge into a 'we'
And not a 'me and you'.

No star, no leaf should fall
Without your falling too.
They'll rise up one and all
Each hour, and so will you.

AUTUMN COMES EARLY

The pungent smell of dead leaves fills the air;
The cornfields now are desolate and bare.
We know that when the wild winds come to play
They'll blow our weary summer on its way.

The gorse bush crackles. Suddenly it will see
That all the things we think we're holding fast
Have faded to a dim and distant past
And every flower was just a wondrous dream.

The frightened soul sends out this wish to me—
That to the present it should cease to cling
That it should face its fading, like a tree
That autumn too its festive fare might bring.

[THE FRENZY OF THE BOOM
AND THE FEVER OF PROPERTY
SPECULATION]

WHEN, AFTER A WORLD WAR and many personal misfortunes, I came to Montagnola forty years ago, shipwrecked but ready to battle on and start afresh, it was just a sleepy little village in the midst of vineyards and forests of chestnut trees. And that was how it remained for many years. Until our hill also found itself in that state—or that sickness—which Knut Hamsun has described with such uncanny vividness in *Children of the Age* and *Segelfoss Town*. Where yesterday a whimsically winding path had climbed the slope and disappeared among rows of vines and honeysuckle hedges, today above the churned-up mounds of earth one could see lorries stopping and discharging their loads of bricks and their bags of cement, and then a little later, instead of wildflowers, vines and fig trees, there were wire fences with shrill-coloured little suburban houses behind them. Creeping up from the town and the valley, getting relentlessly closer and closer to us, came building plots, new houses, streets, walls, cement mixers, the frenzy of the boom and the fever of property speculation. It was the death of the forest, the meadows, the vineyards. The machines of the building industry rumbled and roared, and the riveting hammers banged on the oil tanks. No one could object—the people were in the right; decades ago I too had fenced off a piece of land, had planted a hedge round it and had built a house and a garden and paths. Of course at that time I was not one of the 'children of the age' so much as an individual eccentric who settled down far from the village, planted trees, battled against the weeds and looked down somewhat scornfully on the town and its little suburbs. The scorn had long since faded, our little village had turned into a Segelfoss town, and house by house, street by street it grew bigger, shops were opened or extended, there was a new post office, a café, a newspaper kiosk, a hundred new telephone connections, and our former walks disappeared, as did my hidden painting spots and resting places from my Klingsor time. The great wave had reached us, and ours was no longer a village, and our surroundings no longer the countryside. And no matter how remote and hidden our house had been when we built it nigh on thirty years ago, now the surge was lapping at our feet, and field after field was sold, plotted, built on and fenced off. We were still protected by our situation on the steep slope and on a rough and narrow track, but the terraced fields below our property, with their few vineyards and trees and their picturesque old stable, were already attracting prospective buyers, some wanting to build and others to speculate, and every so often one could see strangers clambering around, testing, contemplating the view, pacing here and there to measure distances. Tomorrow or the day after, these remnants of tranquillity and nature would be taken from us. And it wasn't just a matter of us two old folk and our peace and quiet, but also of that which our lords and masters had built, planted and established here and had left to us as their vassals, and of that which now we would assuredly no longer be able to give back as we had found it.

From Bericht an Freunde
(Report to Friends) *1959*

The world does not give us very much now; it often seems to consist of nothing but noise and fear, and yet grass and trees still grow. And if one day the whole world should be covered with concrete boxes, the clouds will still be playing up above, and here and there people will still, with the help of art, be holding open a door to the divine.

From an undated letter

161

LADY WORLD, FAREWELL

In shreds the world's now lying
Though once we loved her dear
But now the thought of dying
For us holds little fear.

She should not feel our rages
So wild and bright is she
And the magic of the ages
Still colours all we see.

But gladly we'll be leaving
Her game. We'll say adieu
To all the joy and grieving
To all the loving too.
Lady World, farewell now
Be young and lovely still
But of your heaven and hell now
We have had our fill.

Of course one must differentiate between the resignation of the tired old man, who no longer has much interest in the world, and the actual, innermost beliefs of that old man. The tiredness after all is only something physiological, and if I am happy to leave this present world with all its stench, that does not mean that I despair of the world and humankind now and for ever. I sense destruction and I see the ugliest things approaching, but they will also come to an end, and in a world that has been totally destroyed, everything good for which man has the potential and the desire may blossom once again.

From a letter written in
October 1951 to Georg Schwarz

There is no loftier spectacle than the man who has become wise and has thrown off the shackles of the temporal and the personal.

From an undated letter

SOMETIMES

Sometimes when the wind is howling
Or a songbird sings its song
Or a dog barks in the distance
I stay still and listen long.

My soul flies back a thousand years
To a past long left behind
When the singing bird and the howling wind
And I were brothers, all one kind.

My soul's an animal, a tree
A cloud that's drifting in the sky.
A stranger, changed, it now returns

And asks me. How should I reply?

[A CALL FROM BEYOND CONVENTION]

RECENTLY A YOUNG MAN who wrote to me addressed me as "old and wise". "I trust your judgement," he wrote, "because you are old and wise." I was in the midst of one of my brighter moments, and instead of reading the letter—which, incidentally, was very similar to hundreds that I get from other people—in every detail, I fished out the odd words and sentences from here and there, looked at them as closely as possible, and asked them exactly what was their essential meaning. "Old and wise" stood there, and that might make a tired and grumpy old man laugh, who throughout his long and rich life had very often thought he was immeasurably closer to wisdom than he was now, in his reduced and none too cheerful condition. Old, yes, that I was, it's true—old, worn out, disillusioned and tired. And yet the word 'old' could also express something completely different! When we talked of old tales, old houses and towns, old trees, old communities, old forms of worship, there was absolutely nothing belittling, derogatory or disdainful in the term. And so even the qualities of age were something I could only partially attribute to myself—of the many meanings of the word, I was inclined to accept and apply to myself only the negative ones. But for the young correspondent, for all I knew the word 'old' could have a picturesque, grey-bearded, gently smiling, partly moving, partly venerable value and sense—at least it had always had these associations for me in the days when I myself was not old. All right, then, one could accept the word, understand it and respect it as a mode of address.

But now for the word 'wise'! Well, what exactly was it supposed to mean? If what it was supposed to mean was a nothing—just a general, vague, conventional epithet, an expression, then one could leave it out altogether. But if it wasn't a nothing, if it really was supposed to mean something, how was I to delve down into this meaning? I recalled an old method that I'd often used before—namely, that of free association. I had a little rest, walked round the room a few times, said the word 'wise' out loud again, and waited for the first idea to come into my head. Lo and behold, what arrived was another word—Socrates. Anyway, that was something, and it wasn't just a word, it was a name, and behind the name was not an abstraction but a figure, a person. So what did the flimsy concept of wisdom have to do with the substantial, very real name of Socrates? That was easy to spot. Wisdom was the quality that school and university teachers, famous people lecturing in overflowing halls, authors of leading articles and feature pages invariably latched onto first, the moment they mentioned Socrates. Socrates the Wise. The wisdom of Socrates—or, as the learned lecturer would say, the wisdom of a Socrates. There was nothing more to say about this wisdom. But no sooner would one have heard the expression than no doubt there would arise a reality, a truth—the real Socrates. A truly mighty and, despite all the legends draped round him, a truly convincing figure. And this figure, this old Athenian with the nicely ugly face had provided unmistakable information about his own wisdom, because he had expressly and emphatically announced that he knew nothing, absolutely nothing, and had absolutely no claim whatsoever to the attribute of wisdom …

And so there I stood, a wise old man, before the unwise old Socrates, and must either defend myself or feel ashamed. There was more than enough reason to be ashamed, because regardless of all the fiddling and the hair-splitting I knew perfectly well that the young man who had called me wise had by no means done so out of stupidity or youthful innocence, but that I had given him the opening, had seduced him, had more or less authorised him to do so through my literary writings—in which something like experience and reflection, something like a lesson and the wisdom of age might be sensed—and although, I believe, later on in my state of doubt I had put most of my literary 'pearls of wisdom' in quotation marks, or even changed or rescinded them, nevertheless when all is said and done I had throughout my life and work said yes more often than no, accepted or kept quiet instead of fought, and all too frequently paid my respects to the traditions of the mind, of faith, of language, of convention. In my writings, it was undeniable that one could sense here and there a glimmer of light, a break in the clouds and in the drapery of the traditional altarpiece, a crack behind which there was some threatening, ghostly, apocalyptic vision—the occasional suggestion that man's most secure possession was his poverty, and his most actual bread his hunger; but all in all, like everyone else I had preferred to embrace the beautiful worlds of form and tradition, and had chosen to walk in the gardens of sonatas and fugues and symphonies rather than those of the apocalyptic fiery furnaces, and I had opted for the enchanting games and comforts of language rather than for all those experiences in which language comes to an end and turns to nothingness because, for a terrifying or beautiful, perhaps blessed or perhaps fatal moment, we are confronted by the inexpressible, the unthinkable, the very heart of the world, which can only be glimpsed as a mystery or as a wound. If the young letter-writer had seen in me, not an ignorant Socrates but a wise man in the sense of the professors and the critics, then by and large I had indeed given him the right to do so ...

This analysis of the words "old and wise" had therefore been of little use. Now, in order somehow to have done with the letter, I took the opposite route and instead of looking to gain enlightenment from various individual words, I turned to the content, for the overall purpose of which the young man had written his letter. This purpose was a question—an apparently very simple question, and therefore conducive to an apparently very simple answer. The question was: "Does life have a meaning, and would it not be better to put a bullet in one's head?" At first sight, this question would not seem to permit a wide variety of answers. I could reply: No, dear boy, life has no meaning and indeed it would be better etc. Or

I could say: Life, dear boy, certainly has a meaning, and there is no question of opting out with a bullet. Or: Although life has no meaning, that is no reason to shoot oneself dead. Or: Life does indeed have its good meaning, but it's so difficult to do it justice or even to know what it is that it would probably be a good idea to put a bullet etc.

These, as one might think initially, would be possible answers to send to the young man. But hardly have I begun to try out other ideas when I see almost immediately that there are not four or eight but hundreds and thousands of answers. And yet, one could swear, for this letter and its writer there is basically only one answer, only one door to freedom, only one salvation from the hell of his distress.

In the search for this one answer, wisdom and old age are no use at all. The question asked by this letter plunges me into total darkness, because those wise words I have at my disposal, and those wise words that far older and far more experienced pastors have at their disposal, work wonderfully well in books and sermons, lectures and essays, but not in this one real-life case, not for this one bona fide patient, who even though he overestimates the value of age and wisdom, is in deadly earnest and has knocked all my weapons, dodges and devices out of my hand with the simple words: "I trust your judgement."

How, then, is this letter, with a question that is as childish as it is earnest, to be answered?

From this letter something flies out at me, something flashes, and I feel and process it more with my nerves than with my reason, more with my gut and my sympathetic nerve than with my experience and wisdom—a breath of reality, a thunderbolt from a gaping hole in the clouds, a call from beyond convention and comfort, and there is no other solution than either to do nothing and keep quiet, or obey and accept the call. Perhaps I still have a choice; perhaps I can still say to myself: There's nothing I can do for the poor boy, I know as little as he does, maybe I can shove the letter right at the bottom of a pile of other letters and semi-consciously make sure it stays at the bottom and gradually disappears until it has been forgotten. But even as I'm thinking this, I already know that I shall only be able to forget it once I've actually answered it, and answered it properly. The fact that I know this, and that I am convinced of it, does not arise out of experience and wisdom, but from the power of the call, from the encounter with reality. It comes from the power which I will draw on for my answer—not from me, from experience, from intelligence, from practice, from humaneness, but from reality itself, from that tiny splinter of reality which this letter has brought to me. The power, then, which will answer this letter lies in the letter itself; it will answer itself; the young man himself will give himself the answer. If he strikes a spark from me, the stone, the wise old man, it will be his hammer, his blow, his problem, his power alone that will ignite the fire.

I should not conceal the fact that I have received this letter with the same question many, many times, and have read it and answered it or not answered it. Only the power of the crisis is not always the same; it is not only strong, pure souls that ask such questions at some time or the other, but there are also rich young folk with their mixture of suffering and devotion. Some have written that I am the one in whose hands they place the decision; a yes from me and they'll recover, a no from me and they'll die—and for all the force of the ultimatum, I could sense that this was just an appeal to my vanity, to my own weakness, and I made my decision—this letter-writer will neither recover because of my yes, nor die because of my no, but will continue to cultivate his problems and maybe send his question to other so-called wise old men, comfort himself and even amuse himself a little with the answers, collect them and put them in a folder.

If I don't think that of today's letter-writer, but

take him seriously, respond to his trust and genuinely want to help him, it's not happening through me but through him—it is his power that's guiding my hand, his reality that's breaking through my conventional old man's wisdom, his purity that is compelling my integrity, not because of some virtue, some neighbourly love, some humanitarian feeling, but for the sake of life and reality, just as when we have breathed out, no matter what may be our purposes and our world views, after a short while we will of necessity have to breathe in again. We don't do it—it just happens to us.

And so now, seized by the need, irradiated by the lightning bolt of real life, I allow myself to be forced by the almost unbearable thinness of the air to act swiftly, and I no longer have doubts or scruples concerning this letter, I no longer subject it to analysis and diagnosis, but I must obey the call, and I do not have to offer my counsel or my knowledge, but must give the one thing that can help—namely, the answer the young man seeks and which he only needs to hear from the lips of another in order to feel that it is his own answer, his own necessity which he himself has conjured up.

It requires a great deal for a letter, a stranger's question, actually to reach the recipient, because the letter-writer—no matter how real and urgent may be his need—can only express himself through conventional signs. He asks: "Does life have a meaning?" and that sounds vague and silly, like a teenager's world-weariness. But he doesn't mean life in the sense of philosophies, dogmas or human rights— he means his own life and his alone, and from my supposed wisdom he does not want to hear some moral platitude or instructions in the art of giving life a meaning. No, he wants his real problem to be viewed by a real person who will share it with him for a moment and thus, for the time being, help him overcome it. And if I give him this help, it won't be me that has helped him, but it will be the reality of his need, which for an hour strips this wise old man of his age and wisdom, and douses him with a glowing, ice-cold wave of reality.

From Geheimnisse (Secrets) *1947*

Old age is not an enemy that one could fight or even shame—it is a mountain landslide that envelops us, a slowly creeping gas that stifles us.

From a letter written on
26th December 1939 to Rolf Schott

END OF AUGUST

In all its glory summer is returning
Although we'd thought that we must say goodbye.
Compressed into the shorter days, it's burning.
The sun is shining from a cloudless sky.

So might a man, leaving all stress and strife
And disillusioned, suddenly once more
Finding himself upon a sandy shore
Risk a dive into the waves of life.

Whether this time on a love affair he'll spend
Or writing some late literary treasure
As clear as autumn in his work or pleasure
Will shine his deep awareness of the end.

Being ill and dying should be the province only of old people, not of those who are still young, strong and happy. One bristles at it, one is shocked and one finds it brutal and unnatural, because humans know through their reason that nature does not by any means act in a friendly or considerate manner, but generally they still cling to the gentle, more pleasant sides of nature and try to envisage her as mother, guardian and friend of the living. When she then shatters the beautiful façade and strikes one of us with her paw, it is always like a terrible, violent awakening from cherished habits and illusions.

From a letter written on
23rd August 1947 to Otto Basler

Being left behind, having fought one's way through life, is also something, and it smacks of a crooked branch waving from an old tree.

From a letter written on
17th October 1928 to Manuel Gasser

Brother Body is often a tiresome because all too close relative. And the 'Conquest of the World' is not a condition but an action, even a battle, in which one does not always come out on top.

From a letter written in July/August
1962 to Gertrud von le Fort

I would like to wish you strength and patience in the struggle with old age, in which one can also gain victory in defeat.

From a postcard written c1950 to Siegfried Seeger

THE FLOWERING BRANCH

To and fro, to and fro
The flowering branch blows wild
Up above and down below
My heart swings like a child
Between the darkness and the light
Between dejection and delight.

Until the blossoms blow away
Until the branch with fruit is blessed
Until the heart at last can rest
Weary of its childish play
Life's hectic game, it will maintain
Was full of joy and was not played in vain.

AUTUMNAL EXPERIENCES

THIS YEAR'S INCOMPARABLE SUMMER—a year which for me overflowed with gifts, celebrations, heart-warming experiences, but also with problems and with work—began to lose some of its friendly, congenial, cheerful *ambiance* towards the end; it descended into patches of melancholy, of irritation and listlessness, and of satiety and readiness to die. If one went to bed at night with the stars at their brightest in heaven, one sometimes awoke in the morning to a thin, grey, tired and sickly light, the terrace was wet and spread its cold dampness all around, the sky let its shapeless clouds hang loosely deep down into the vales, ready at any moment to discharge new showers of rain, and the world, which so recently had been breathing in the abundance and the certainty of summer, smelt harshly and bitterly of autumn, of decay and death, even though the forests and even the grassy slopes, which at this time of year are normally burnt brown and yellow, were still a solid green. It had fallen ill, our normally so robust and reliable late summer; it had grown tired and moody, and it was sinking. But it was still alive. Almost all these fits of indolence, self-neglect and moroseness were followed by a rally and a blossoming, an effort to return to the lovely day before yesterday, and these times of resurrection—they were often no more than hours—had a special, touching, almost timid beauty, a transfigured September smile which was a wonderful mixture of summer and autumn, strength and weariness, will to live and weakness. On some days, this aged summer beauty slowly, pausing for breath, pausing with exhaustion, fought its way through, and hesitantly the excessively clear, gentle light would conquer the horizon and the mountain tops, and in the evening the world and the sky lay in still and tranquil contentment, cool and limpid, promising yet more bright days to come. But overnight it all disappeared again, and in the morning the wind would sweep great gusts of rain over the dripping countryside; gone and forgotten were the cheerful, promising smiles of the evening, the scents and colours were washed away, the bright boldness and the all-conquering courage of yesterday's battle were now submerged in waves of weariness.

It was not only for my own sake that I regarded these strangely eccentric switches and swings with mistrust and a degree of unease. And it was not only my own everyday existence that was threatened by these intrusions, which required that I should for a time remain shut up in my house and in my living room. There was also an important event coming up for which a friendly sky and a certain amount of warmth seemed more than desirable—the visit of a dear old friend from Swabia. This visit, already postponed several times, was due to take place in just a few days. Although my friend only intended to be my guest for one solitary evening, it would be a sad loss for me if his arrival, stay and departure had to take place in dark and miserable weather. And so I watched the sicknesses and recoveries, the restless ups and downs of the weather with great concern. My son, who was keeping me company during my wife's long absence, helped me in the forest and vineyard, I performed my daily household duties, also chose a present for my eagerly awaited visitor, and in the evening I told my son a little bit about him—about our friendship, about his character and his work, for in the land of the knowledgeable my friend was the heir and the embodiment of all the best traditions, honoured and loved as one of the country's great and good. How sad I would be if Otto, who to my knowledge had not been to the south for decades and who had never seen my house, my garden, or my view over the lake and valley, should observe all this while shivering in the damp dark light of a rainy autumn day. But secretly I was torn and tormented by a very different thought, a strangely inhibiting and embarrassing thought—my childhood friend, first a lawyer, then Lord Mayor of a city, then for a while a public servant, then in retirement loaded with all sorts of honorary positions—some important—had never lived in very comfortable let alone luxurious surroundings, and under Hitler's regime as a civil servant who refused to toe the line, he and his large family had endured a period of hunger; then came the war, the bombings, the loss of his home and all his possessions, and yet with courage and cheerful acceptance he had coped with a Spartan life, having few personal needs; and so how would it seem to him, finding me, who had been spared the war, living in a spacious and prosperous house, with two studies, servants and many comforts that I could scarcely do without, but which would appear to him like the luxuries of a bygone age? Of course he already knew a certain amount about my life, and that all these nice, maybe luxurious things had been bought or given to me after long years of sacrifice and deprivation. But all the same, although my prosperity would not arouse any envy in him, perhaps the most honourable of all my friends, nevertheless he would eventually have to suppress a smile seeing all the superfluous and unnecessary things which he would find in my home and which I would regard as necessities. Life takes you along strange paths—once I had a lot of inhibitions and complexes because I was poor and my trousers were ragged, whereas now I was embarrassed by my possessions and comforts.

I told my son when and where we two friends had first got to know each other. Sixty-one years ago— it was also in September—we had been taken as schoolchildren by our mothers to the monastery at Maulbronn; I have described it in detail in one of my books. There Otto and I were classmates, though he wasn't yet my friend. That didn't come about until we met again later on, but the friendship that grew from this became firm, unsentimental and warm. My friend had a direct and strong connection with literature, inherited from a learned and cultured father and fostered and nourished all through his life; this made him receptive to the work and character of a writer to whom he was already linked by shared memories. And as far as I was concerned, this friend was to be admired and sometimes even envied for his solid roots in a homeland with all its traditions,

which endowed an already calm and stable being with
a broad, secure base in which I myself was lacking.
He was far removed from any form of nationalism,
and perhaps even more sensitive in his opposition
to patriotic fervour and hysteria than I was, but he
was completely at home in his Swabia, its landscapes
and history, its language and literature, its store of
wise sayings and traditions, and what had begun as
a natural heritage—his familiarity with the secrets,
the laws of growth and life as well as the diseases
and dangers of this native folklore—had developed
over decades of study and experience into a wealth
of knowledge that was the envy of many a patriotic
orator. For me at any rate, as an outsider, he was the
personification of all that was good about Swabia.

And so, at last, he arrived, and the grand reunion
got underway. He had grown a little older and his
movements a little slower since our last meeting, but as
on every previous occasion he seemed to me remark-
ably fit and strong for his age—which was the same as
mine—and he stood firm on his well-practised hiker's
legs, so that as always I felt somewhat weak and shaky
by comparison. And he did not come without a gift for
his host. As an emissary from my Swabian relatives,
he brought with him a heavy packet containing all the
letters which had survived from my correspondence

with my sister Adele between *circa* 1890 and 1948. Thus he brought me not only the chance to conjure up the past in our own conversation, but also a veritable treasure trove of the past condensed into all these documents. Although the little gift I had got for him now seemed thoroughly trivial, from the very moment of his arrival I no longer felt the slightest sense of embarrassment, and I happily and with a clear conscience showed him round my house. We took pleasure in each other's company, he was in the best of moods after his trip, and from my point of view, my guest had brought back a part of my boyhood and of my childhood home. I also managed to dissuade him from his intention to leave the next morning—he agreed to postpone his departure for a day. He treated my son with the friendly courtesy of an old gentleman who, at the age of seventy-five, is not in the least put out but genuinely pleased to make a new acquaintance. Martin too could sense that he was privileged to be meeting someone of very special qualities, and several times when we were standing talking outside the house, he crept up on us with his camera and photographed us.

Very few of those for whom I am writing this account are as old as I am. Most of them don't know what it can mean to old people—especially when they have spent their lives far from the places and images of their youth—to see an object that bears witness to the reality of those earlier times: an old piece of furniture, a faded photograph, a letter the sight of whose handwriting and paper opens up and illuminates whole treasure chambers of past life, and in which we rediscover nicknames and colloquialisms that no one would understand today, and the sound and meaning of which we ourselves must make an enjoyable little effort to bring back into our memory. But it means much more, so much more than such documents from distant times to be reunited with a living person with whom you were once together as boy and youth, and who knew your long since dead and buried teachers, and has even preserved memories of them that you yourself have forgotten. We look at each other, my schoolmate and I, and what we see is not just the white hair and the tired eyes under the creased and somewhat stiffened eyelids; behind today, we see the yesteryear; we are not two old men talking to each other, but we are also seminarist Otto talking to seminarist Hermann, and beneath all the many layers of years, each of us can see the fourteen-year-old schoolboy, hear his boy's voice of the time, see him sitting on his bench pulling faces, see him playing ball games or running, with hair flying and eyes flashing, see on the still childish face the first dawnings of enthusiasm, of emotion and of incipient awareness of intellect and beauty.

Let me digress. Old people often develop a sense of history that they didn't have in their youth, and this arises out of their knowledge of these many layers, which in the course of decades of experience and suffering merge into a human face and a human mind. Basically, even if not always consciously, all old people think historically. They are not content with the surface layer, which suits young people so well. They would not like to be without it, or to erase it, but beneath it they also like to perceive the consequences of their layers of experience, which only the present can endow with their full significance.

To continue—our first evening was a veritable feast. We talked not only of our youthful memories, and about the lives, health or recent deaths of our schoolmates in Maulbronn, but we also discussed and confessed all kinds of things—matters Swabian and German, the cultural life over there, the deeds and problems of important contemporaries. For the most part, our conversations were cheerful, and even very serious topics were broached with a kind of playful detachment, which is a natural and easily digestible way for us old folk to deal with current affairs. But for

me, the recluse, it was all unusually exciting; we stayed
at table far longer than usual, talked and listened for
three hours on end, and my heart was warmed by
all the news from my former home, and I had been
enticed deep into the jungles of memory; I could
sense in advance that all this would be followed by
a bad night, and I was not wrong. But I was happy
and willing to pay such a price for this wonderful
experience. However, the next morning I was ill and
exhausted, and glad that my helpful and affectionate
son was there beside me. My friend was as relaxed
and cheerful as ever; I had never seen him ill, nervous, moody or overtired. Throughout the morning
I did absolutely nothing, took a powder, and from
midday onwards was once more ready for action.
The weather was bright, and I was able to invite my
guest to make a tour of our hill. I felt neither ashamed
nor envious to see that he was so fit, had slept well,
and was responsive to everything I showed him; on
the contrary, it did me good, because this dear man
had an aura of calm and classical ataraxia which I
was delighted and grateful to perceive, and to allow
to take its effect on me as well. How good and fine
and right it was that the two of us were so different
in temperament, constitution and talents! Or rather,
how fine it was that each of us had stayed true to his

own person, and had become exactly what nature had made him—the serene but indefatigable civil servant with a deep love of literature and scholarship, and the nervous, all too easily wearied and yet secretly tough man of letters. All in all, each of us had more or less achieved and realised everything he could have asked of himself and everything he owed to the world. Perhaps Otto had had the happier life, but neither of us paid much attention to 'happiness', or at least it had not been the goal of our aspirations.

In one respect, I had an advantage over him. I was three months older, and my seventy-fifth birthday celebrations were behind me—I had got through it all, delivered my thanks, and the understanding organisers had given me special dispensation from making personal appearances at the celebrations. But he, my valiant Swabian, still had all of this to come, without any such dispensation, and in the near future he would have to face all the festive stresses and strains, which would be far from minor because all kinds of honours were to be showered upon him. There was also a little birthday present from me, already in the hands of a mutual friend in Stuttgart—a small, illuminated manuscript. No doubt he would cope far better than me with what lay ahead, and would know how to respond with dignity and charm to the ceremonies, allocutions, awards, and would conscientiously return the hundreds of bows and handshakes. Even if he had not been so exposed to the spotlight as I had, nevertheless his life had not been guided by the aphorism "*Bene vixit qui bene latuit*"*; he was a very well-known man who presumably had other enemies apart from the Nazis and had survived many a battle, but who now in the evening of his loyal, hard-working life was—in the eyes of those who knew about such things—one of the most indispensable representatives of the Swabian mind and spirit. We didn't speak of these approaching times of honour, but we talked about those institutions of local cultural life that had given such vital support to his work during the dark days, and indeed had saved it. We also talked a little about our wives, and in particular the fact that his had recently been ill, and mine had for a few weeks been away on a well-earned holiday, fulfilling a long-held dream by going to Ithaca, Crete and Samos.

Our second and last evening was also one of complete pleasure and harmony, producing a whole new range of items from the treasure chest of memory, plus many a wise word gleaned from my friend's experiences. He was too conscientious and too great a lover of language ever to be a showy conversationalist, but

* *He who was well hidden had a good life.* Ovid

he talked without effort, slowly and always choosing his words carefully. Later than intended, we eventually said goodbye, as he wanted to leave next morning at an hour when my day has not yet even begun, and I could rely on my son to do the honours. As we took leave of each other, we both smiled without putting into words what we were both thinking: "This is perhaps the last time."

The days grew ever more autumnal, the rainy ones ever darker, the brighter ones ever colder, and there was already snow on many of the hilltops. The Sunday after my guest's departure was particularly beautiful; my son and I drove up to a high point from which we could see the Valais Alps, and in most of the surrounding villages people were still busy with the grape harvest. We enjoyed the vivid scene, and wished my friend could have been with us on this day too, taking in the blue and gold and white of the distant hills, the crystal-clear brightness of the air and the colourful groups of grape-pickers on the vine terraces.

At this very moment, as we were thinking of him on our way, my friend died.

He had reached home safe and sound and happy, had written postcards to several friends, including my sister, telling them about his visit to Montagnola, had also informed me about his safe return, and had thereupon been required to devote all his attention to one of his many offices. And on the very afternoon that had blessed us with its light and shimmering colours, he had felt unwell for just a short while, and then with a minimum of fuss had died. I learnt about it the next morning through a telegram which asked me to write a few words to be spoken at the graveside, and soon afterwards came a short letter from his wife. It said: "At two o'clock yesterday, Sunday, my husband died unexpectedly and without a struggle. He was able to experience friendship and love on his visit to you, and for that I would like to thank you. May you too think of him now with good thoughts."

Oh yes, with all my heart I thought of him. And despite the pain this loss brought me, above all else this death, of a man who in his life had been regarded as a model by so many good and honourable people, seemed to me in itself a wondrous model. To the very last moment he had accepted his responsibilities, faithfully done his work, and then no sickbed, no complaint, no cry for sympathy and attention, but just a simple, quiet, gentle death. A death which, for all one's grief, one had to accept; a death which brought a peaceful end to a life of courage and service, and had kindly spared a friend, who had probably not even realised how tired he was, from the demands of the world and from the stress which his birthday would have imposed on him in just a few days' time.

The fact that for a moment, before he allowed himself to rest, he had called on me, had sat at my table, had brought me greetings and gifts from my home, that perhaps I was the last person with whom he had held a conversation outside the confines of work and everyday life, that he had once more honoured me with his friendship and affection, with his radiant warmth and calm and good humour, was a privilege and a blessing. Without this experience, I would probably not have been able to understand his end, though 'understand' is perhaps not the best word for the acceptance and classification of it as something good, right, harmonious and fitting. May his friends also see it this way, and at times when they and I most need it, may his person, his being, his life and his death be a comfort and an encouraging example to us all.

1952

ON THE NEWS OF
THE DEATH OF A FRIEND

Swiftly the transient fades away.
Swiftly the withered years depart.
With scorn the stars look down, seeming eternal.

Deep within us only the spirit
Impassively can watch this game
Not with scorn, not with pain.
For 'transient' and 'eternal'
Mean as much, mean as little …

However, the heart
Resists and glows with love
Yielding like a fading flower
To the endless call of death
To the endless call of love.

In growing old, one has a tendency to take moral appearances, confusion and degeneration in the lives of individuals and of nations as whims of nature, although at least one is left with the comforting prospect that after every disaster the grass and flowers will grow again, and that after every fit of madness, nations will return to certain basic moral needs within which, in spite of everything, there seems to be an innate stability and normality.

From a letter written on
14th June 1939 to Helene Welti

During our conversation, [Rudolf Alexander] Schröder came up with an unforgettable remark. He was talking about age and growing old (which does me no good, and leaves a bad taste). After he'd delivered something like a song of praise to life, he bent over very close to my face, with a radiant smile, and whispered with delight: "With old age things get more and more beautiful."

From a letter written in
April 1952 to Georg von der Vring

A WALK IN LATE AUTUMN

Autumn rains have stirred the forest grey
The valley shivers in the morning wind
And from the chestnut tree the fruits crash down
Burst open, with laughter moist and brown.

My life has been disturbed by autumn too
The wind has ripped the shredded leaves away
And rattles branch by branch—where is the fruit?

I blossomed love, and yet the fruit was pain
I blossomed faith, and yet the fruit was hate.
The wind is tearing at my dried-up branches.
I laugh at it. I can withstand such storms.

What's fruit to me? What's purpose! Once I blossomed
And blossom was my purpose. Now I fade
And fading is my purpose, nothing else
For short-term are the purposes of the heart.

God lives in me, God dies in me, God suffers
Within my breast, and that's sufficient purpose.
Right path or wrong, whether fruit or blossom
All is one, for all are merely names.

The valley shivers in the morning wind
And from the chestnut trees the fruits crash down
With laughter hard and bright. And I laugh with them.

This collapse into old age has its good side, because it makes us doubly indifferent to what goes on outside— to world history and to the joint-stock companies that drive it on.

> *From a letter written c1950 to Otto Basler*

Moving house gets more and more difficult with age, and in the end a hearse is more welcome than a removal van.

> *From a letter written on 15th April 1931 to Helene Welti*

One becomes so undemanding in old age that if one has had a good night's sleep and no severe pain, one is almost happy.

From a letter written in late August 1948 to Hans Huber

[THE TENDENCY TOWARDS FIXED HABITS AND REPETITIONS]

SOMETHING ELSE … is the way old people experience things, and here I don't wish to and mustn't allow myself to indulge in fiction or illusion, but will stick to my knowledge of the fact that a person of younger or even youthful years has no idea of the way old people do experience things. For basically, there are no new experiences left for them; they have long since lived through all the appropriate, predetermined primary experiences, and their 'new' ones—which become rarer and rarer—are repetitions of those they have already had sometimes or often; new varnish on a painting apparently finished long ago, a new layer of paint or gloss, one layer over ten, over a hundred earlier layers. And yet they do mean something new, and although they are not primary, nevertheless they are real experiences. Because every time, among other things they become encounters with oneself and examinations of oneself. The man who sees the ocean for the first time or hears *Figaro* for the first time experiences something different and generally more intense than the man who does so for the tenth or fiftieth time. Because the latter has different, less active but more experienced and more sharply honed eyes and ears for the ocean or the music, and he not only feels the no longer new impression differently and more discerningly than the other, but with this repetition he is also reminded of the earlier occasions, and so as well as experiencing the already familiar ocean and music in a new way, he also encounters himself again, his younger self, and the many earlier stages of his life within the framework of that experience—regardless of whether he does so with a smile, a sneer, a superior sniff, emotion, embarrassment, joy or regret. In general, the older a person is, the more he is inclined to view his earlier exploits and experiences with emotion or embarrassment rather than with feelings of superiority, and that applies particularly to creative people like artists, who in the later stages of life, on being reunited with the power, intensity and richness of their peak years will very rarely get the feeling: "Oh, how weak and stupid I was in those days!" On the contrary, they are more liable to wish: "Oh, if only I had a bit of the energy I had then!"

We poets and intellectuals attach a great deal of importance to memory—it is our capital and we live on it, but when we are surprised by an intrusion from the underworld of the forgotten and the discarded, it is always the discovery, whether pleasant or not, of a powerful force which does not reside within the memories of ourselves that we have so carefully nurtured. Occasionally I have had the thought or the suspicion that it might be the desire to wander free and to conquer the world, the hunger for the new, the not yet seen, for travel and for the exotic, that is familiar to most people with a bit of imagination, especially when they are young, and also a longing to be forgotten, to drive away what has been, in so far as it oppresses us, and to cover the images we know with as many new images as possible. On the other hand, the tendency of old age to cling to fixed habits and repetitions, to go back again and again to the same areas, people and situations would then be a striving after memories, a never satisfied need to reassure oneself concerning what memory has preserved, together perhaps with a desire, a mild hope, that one might see this preserved treasure expand, perhaps one day to rediscover this or that experience, this or that encounter, this or that image or face which had been lost and forgotten, and thus to add to the

HERMANN HESSE

store of memories. All old people, even if they are not aware of it, are in search of the past, the seemingly irretrievable which is not, however, irretrievable and not necessarily gone for ever, because under certain conditions—for instance, through literature—it can be restored and for ever torn away from the grasp of the past.

From the circular letter Engadiner
Erlebnisse (Engadine Experiences)
1953

Truth is a typical ideal of young people, whereas love is one for mature people and for those who take pains to prepare themselves for decline and death. For thinking people, the urgent quest for truth only ceases when they have realised that man is extraordinarily badly equipped for the recognition of objective truth, so that searching for it really can't be the activity for us humans. But even those who never actually achieve such insights go through the same process of discovery in the course of their unconscious experiences. Possessing the truth, being right, knowing, being able to distinguish precisely between good and evil, and consequently judging, punishing, condemning, being able and allowed to wage war—this is for young people and it suits young people too. As one gets older and comes to a standstill in the face of these ideals, so the ability—which in any case is pretty feeble—that we humans have, to 'awaken' and to sense superhuman truths, simply fades away.

From a letter written in June 1931 to Fanny Schiler

Age and calcification are advancing; sometimes the blood doesn't want to flow through the brain as it should. But when all is said and done, these evils also have their good side—one doesn't take things in so clearly or so intensely any more, one misses a lot, one no longer even feels various blows and pinpricks, and a part of the person that was once called me is already there where soon the whole will be.

From Ein Brief nach Deutschland (A Letter to Germany) *1946*

It's one of the few good things about old age that one can't be so completely touched by the present and reality any more, because there's a slowly thickening veil coming between us.

From a letter written on 7th September 1951 to Ludwig Tügel

Nowadays when one is old, one lives on a different geological level with a different climate and in a completely different environment from that in which one grew up and which was once normal and natural. At times one is amazed that one is actually still here.

From a letter written in February 1950 to Jeanne Berta Semmig

THE PATH TO LONELINESS

The world falls away
All joys burn out
That once you loved;
The ashes threaten darkness.

Into yourself
You sink, reluctantly
Pushed by a stronger hand;
Freezing, you stand in a world that now is dead;
Drifting towards you here, and weeping
The dying sounds of your lost home
Of children's voices, tender tones of love.

Hard is the path to loneliness.
Harder than you ever thought
And the source of dreams is dry.
Have faith, though! At the end
Of this your path, there will be a home
Death and rebirth
The grave, the eternal Mother.

[HAVING REACHED VERY OLD MANHOOD]

BETWEEN THE OLD and the very old there is a strange relationship. At least this is how it is with me—when a younger friend or colleague surprises me with the fact that suddenly he is sixty or seventy, has heart problems and has had to give up smoking, or has been made an honorary doctor, honorary president or freeman of the city, or has been assailed by one of the many other symptoms of old age, I am quite shocked by the perception that someone whose youthful follies we have just been looking upon with mild indulgence has suddenly claimed his place among the grown-ups and the dignitaries and, with grey or white hair, has entered the realm of old age, complete with honorary titles and decorations. With the stubbornness of my advanced years I had subconsciously expected, and indeed relied upon the fact, that the younger man would remain young and would keep me for ever in touch with young people.

Once I have got over this first little shock, then of course I no longer consider the younger person's moving-along process to be something audacious and even presumptuous, but instead begin to feel a degree of sympathy for the now old; that is to say, with the facts having shown themselves to be unalterable, my old man's stubbornness immediately establishes a distance between myself and my younger friend. Because, I assume in the darkness of my senility, these symptoms that accompany the arrival of a greater age—birthdays and honours as well as aches and pains—still have the gloss of something new, the importance of a first experience, with the seventieth birthday boy feeling rather like the newly confirmed or the newly graduated; a new stage has been reached, a new room has been entered; the sense of resignation mingles pleasantly with the scent of ceremony—there will presumably be a celebratory feast with saddle of venison, burgundy and champagne, and the happy new arrival will still take it all fairly seriously, will listen not without emotion to the speech by the Minister of State or the Lord Mayor, will look back not without melancholy at the harmless high spirits of earlier celebrations and so, as I ascertain with some smugness, will therefore still be a youngster and a beginner by comparison with those of us who are really

old. For those of us who are really old imagine that
we have transcended all these vanities and, in cool
proximity to death, now live a life of wisdom and
dignified renunciation, and only rarely in our especially enlightened moments do we realise how slight
is the difference between being very old and being
old, and between our wisdom and the illusions and
vanities which we short-sightedly attribute to those
who are not yet standing at the same lofty heights as
ourselves. And in these enlightened moments, we also
recall how once as children or boys or teenagers we
thought and laughed about the old and the very old,
and we know that this laughter was far from being
as innocent and silly as we might, even after many
decades, have liked to think it was. Indeed we know
that ultimately the only wisdom of age that has any
substance consists in once more becoming a child.

It is with such thought games that I generally react
when I hear news of sixtieth, seventieth or seventy-fifth
birthdays within the circle of my somewhat younger
friends. They are an attempt to resist with some humour the uneasy feelings that overcome us whenever
we are notified of how swiftly time flies and how fragile
life is. One of the contradictions of this life, whose
tragic aspects are so often and so easily covered up by
its comedy, is the fact that with one half of our souls

215

we artists are delighted by and in love with nothing so much as the moment, the short-lived, the lightning changes of life's directions, while in the other half of our souls we have and nourish the deep desire for permanence, for stasis, for eternity—the longing that goes on driving us to try and achieve the impossible: the spiritualisation and externalisation of the transient, the crystallisation of the fluid and changeable, the capture of the moment. It is what the wise man seeks to attain in his contemplative renunciation of all actions—the cancellation of time—that is what we artists strive for in our reversal of direction; we strain every sinew to keep things firm and fixed for ever.

*From a letter written in November
1957 to Ernst Morgenthaler*

On your entry into a new habitat, the forecourt to old age, an old man wishes you all the gifts that life at this stage has to offer—increased independence from the judgement of others, increased imperviousness to the passions, and an unworried reverence for the eternal.

*A page from an album
written in the 1950s*

We are curious about undiscovered bays in the South Seas, about the earth's polar regions, about the nature of the winds, currents, lightning, avalanches—but we are infinitely more curious about death, the last and boldest adventure of our existence. Because we think we know that of all our insights and experiences, only those for which we willingly sacrifice our lives can be deserving and satisfying.

From Reiselust
(Wanderlust) *1910*

When a person has grown old and has done his all, it is his task peacefully to make friends with death. He does not need other people. He knows them and has seen enough of them. What he needs is peace. It is not seemly to seek out such a person, to talk to him, to torment him with your chatter. At the gateway to his home the proper thing is to pass by, as if nobody lived there.

A notice that Hesse stuck to the door of his house after he had been awarded the Nobel Prize

ON AN AGE-OLD, WEATHER-BEATEN BUDDHA IN A WOODED GORGE IN JAPAN

Softened and smoothed by rains sent down from the skies
Green with moss, by icy frosts deep burned
Your gentle cheeks, your large and lowered eyes
In peace towards their distant goal are turned
Willing to decay and to disperse
Into the shapeless, boundless universe.
Yet still the crumbling posture and expression
Reveal the noble motives of your mission
Seeking, despite the mud, the earth, the chill
The fading forms, your great task to fulfil.
Tomorrow into roots and leaves you'll turn
And into water, reflecting sky and sun
And into ivy, algae and green fern
An image of the eternal All-is-One.

CHINESE PARABLE

An old man named Chunglang, which means 'Master Rock', owned a small farm in the mountains. One day it so happened that one of his horses went missing. Then the neighbours came to offer him their sympathy over this misfortune.

The old man, however, asked them: "How do you know that it's a misfortune?" And lo and behold, a few days later the horse returned and brought with it a whole herd of wild horses. Once again the neighbours came, this time to offer him their congratulations on his good fortune.

The old man from the mountains, however, responded: "How do you know that it's good fortune?"

Since he now had so many horses at his disposal, the son of the old man developed a liking for riding, and one day he broke his leg. Then back they came, the neighbours, in order to express their sympathy. But once again the old man said to them: "How do you know that it's a misfortune?"

The following year, the Commission of 'Beanpoles' came to the mountains to take away tall, strong men to serve the Emperor as boot-men and litter-bearers. They did not take the old man's son, because he still hadn't recovered from his broken leg.

Chunglang could not resist a smile.

THE RAISED FINGER

Master Chu-Chi was, so we are told
A modest, gentle man, not brash or bold;
In words and lectures he did not believe
For words are outward shows that can deceive
And he abhorred deception of all kinds.
When students, monks and novices discussed
With noble words and brilliant flashing minds
The meaning of the world and other teachings
He treated their discussions with mistrust
On silent guard against such overreachings.
Whenever they with many questions came
Some vain, some earnest, all about the meaning
Of ancient writings, or the Buddha's name
About Enlightenment, the world's beginning
And its end, he gave them no reply
But soundlessly would raise his finger high.
The silent eloquence of this finger raised
Grew ever more profound and animated
It talked, it gave instructions, punished, praised
The heart of life and truth it penetrated
And many young men, when this finger spoke
Knew what it meant, and trembled, and awoke.

We have lived through suffering and disease, we have lost friends to death, and death has not only knocked on our window from outside, but it has also done its work inside us and has made progress. Life, which once we took so much for granted, has become a precious but increasingly threatened possession, and what was self-evidently our own has changed into a loan of uncertain duration.

But the loan that may be called in at any time has by no means lost its value—on the contrary, the threat has increased it. We love life just as we did before, and want to remain true to it, for the sake among other things of love and friendship which, down through the years, like wine of good vintage, do not lose but increase their quality and value.

*From a letter written on
24th August 1957 to Max
Wassmer*

The loss of our nearest and dearest, and especially our childhood friends, is one of the many strange and ambivalent experiences that old age puts us through— perhaps the strangest. As gradually everything fades away, and in the end there are far more of those nearest and dearest 'on the other side' than here, one unexpectedly becomes curious about this 'other side', and loses the fear felt by those who are more firmly fenced in.

From a letter written on 17th March 1950 to Thomas Mann

FIRST SNOW

Year, you are old now; once so green and fair
Your looks have faded, snow is in your hair
Your gait is weary, death now walks with you
And so will I, for I am dying too.

Along the fearful path the heart must go
The winter seeds sleep trembling in the snow
The wind has taken from me many a bough
But all the scars are my protection now!
How many bitter times have I been slain!
But with each death, I have been born again.

And so you're welcome, death, gateway of night!
Beyond, life's choir is singing of the light.

I have the same attitude towards death as I had
before—I do not hate it and I do not fear it. If I were
to ask who and what—apart from my wife and my
sons—I love and cherish most, it would transpire that
they are all dead people, the dead of all the centuries,

composers, writers, painters. Their being, compressed into their works, lives on and is more present and real to me than most of my contemporaries. And it is the same with the dead whom I have known, loved and 'lost': my parents and siblings, the friends of my youth—they belong to me and to my life; today just as before, when they were still alive, I think of them, I dream of them, and I regard them as part of my daily life. This attitude towards death is therefore not madness or some sweet fantasy, but is real and integral to my life. I am well acquainted with grief over the transience of things, and I can feel it with every flower that fades. But it is grief without despair.

From a letter written in July 1955
to Hans Bayer

In the last few days I have been reading one of the old Chinese writers—if one calls dead people home-comers, then the living are wanderers. Whoever wanders and does not know where he is going is homeless. If a single person has lost his home, one considers that unfair. But now that the whole world has lost its home, there is no one who would find it unfair.

From an undated letter to Alice Leuthold

Young people like talking about death, but never think about it. With old people it's the other way round. Young people think they will live for ever and so can direct all their wishes and thoughts towards themselves. Old people have realised that somewhere there is an end, and that everything one has and does for oneself ultimately falls into a hole and was for nothing.

From Gertrud, *1909*

.

The dead person was not torn away by chance, or senselessly, or cruelly, or wickedly, but his life's work was over, and he has gone away in order to come back and continue in a new form. 'His work was over' does not, of course, mean that he could not have gone on for many more years achieving valuable things, or that he was replaceable. But for himself, for the innermost meaning of his life, the goal had been reached, he had ripened, and even if he died reluctantly, today he knows it, and of that which he was there is nothing lost or fragmented. That is my belief. There is no death. Every life is eternal, every person returns. There is in every person an innermost self which no death can destroy … I do not believe in a personal reunion, or a return in the form of 'ghosts'. But I believe with all my heart in a common goal for all humans, and in our bond through mind and deed with those who have left us. Not in death but only in life do we find again what is eternal and immortal in the dead.

From a letter written on
30th December 1920 to Anne
Rümelin

To be able to go to sleep when one is tired, and to be able to let fall a burden that one has carried for a long time—that is a precious and wonderful thing.

From Das Glasperlenspiel
(The Glass Bead Game) *1943*

With those whom we can no longer see we commune in a different way than with those who are still 'there'. But they cannot be less present for us, and indeed they are often closer than the others.

From a postcard written in
August 1942 to Lene Gundert

The dear departed, with the essential being that made its impact upon us, remain alive with us so long as we ourselves are alive. Sometimes we can even have a better conversation with them, consult with them, and get better advice from them than from the living.

From a letter written on
4th January 1939 to Lydia Link

Our life is short, and soon we shall be on the other side, and even if we don't 'know' anything about the Great Beyond, nevertheless we have experienced the fact that a dead person may often be dearer and closer to us and more alive than the living all around us, and herein lies the solid foundation of our heart's natural connection with the other side.

From a letter written on 17th May
1947 to Grete Gundert

Every route, whether to the sun or to the night, leads to death, leads to rebirth, of whose pains the soul is afraid. But all follow this path, all die, all are born, for the eternal Mother returns them eternally to the day.

From a letter written in September
1940 to Rolf Conrad

ALL DEATHS

All deaths are deaths that I've already died
All deaths are deaths I wish to die again—
To die the wooden death in the tree
To die the stone death in the mountain
The earthy death in the sand
The crackling death of the leaf in the summer grass
And the bleak and bloody death of the human being.

As a flower I want to be born again
As tree and grass I want to be born again
As fish and deer, as bird and butterfly
And out of every form
My longing will tear each single stage
To the final pains
To the final pains of man.

O bow now drawn and quivering
If the white-knuckled fist of longing
Should seek to bend both poles of life to one!
Then often and over and over again

You will hunt me from death to birth
Along the painful path of creation
Along the glorious path of creation.

The throes of death are also one of life's processes, no less than birth, and often one can confuse the two.

From an undated letter

Pain and lamentation are our first and natural response to the loss of a loved one. They help us through the initial grief and distress, but they are not enough to link us to the dead person.

This is done on a primitive level through the cult of the dead—sacrifices, decorating the grave, monuments, flowers. But at our level, offerings to the dead must take place within our own souls, through thoughts, through the most precise memories, through the reconstruction of the dearly beloved deep within ourselves. If we can accomplish this, the dead person will walk on beside us, his image will be saved and will help us to make our pain fruitful.

From an undated letter

BROTHER DEATH

One day before me you'll appear
To put an end to pain.
You won't forget I'm waiting here
For you to break the chain.

Brother Death, you stand afar
A stranger more or less
Shining like a distant star
Over my distress.

One day, though, you will be near
Burning in my cause.
Come, my brother, I am here
Take me, I am yours.

In recent times I have been given a powerful jolt. Getting old and falling apart, like growing in one's earlier years, occurs in fits and starts. Or rather, it may have proceeded gently and smoothly without one's noticing, but then every so often it suddenly takes a kind of leap, and one becomes very aware of it ... The aches and pains increase, and one often needs all the support of the spirit in order to stand firm.

From a letter written in January 1962 to Felix Lützkendorf

I sometimes think of Regina Ullmann, and imagine her being just as 'busy' as I am and as all very old people are—with weaknesses, with farewells, with fading away. These are processes that require just as much effort as growing and being active, and like all stages of life they have two faces—sometimes they are sad and painful, but sometimes they are positively remarkable, even enjoyable. It changes according to the days and according to the times of day.

From a letter written in March 1958 to Ellen Delp

ONCE, A THOUSAND YEARS AGO

From a broken dream awaking
Restless, longing to take flight
I hear my bamboos softly speaking
Whispering to me in the night.

Instead of gently resting, lying
From old bonds I must break free
Away from here I should be flying
Deep into infinity.

Once, a thousand years ago
There was a home and garden too
Where birds were buried in the snow
Out of which the crocus grew.

I want to break this stifling hold
And spread my wings to fly away
Into those distant times whose gold
Just as brightly shines today.

Until now I had thought little of death, never feared it, often wished for it with desperate impatience. Only now did I see it in all its reality and greatness, how it stands opposite us as a counter-pole, and waits for us so that a destiny can be completed and a circle closed. Until now my life had been a path at whose beginnings I had spent much time surrounded by love, through my mother and my childhood—a path along which I often sang, often sulked, and which also I often cursed, but at no time did I ever see clearly what the end of this path would be. All the effort, all the power that fed my existence seemed to me to proceed from the dark beginnings, from birth and the womb, and death seemed to me to be just the chance point at which all the power, energy and effort would one day be paralysed and extinguished. Only now did I see the greatness and the necessity that lay in this 'chance'. I felt my life to be bound and determined at both ends, and saw my path and my task as being to make my way as to a completion, to ripen, and to approach it as the celebration to end all celebrations.

From Zum Gedächtnis (In Memoriam) *1916*

Anyone who has stepped onto the path of maturity can never lose again, but can only win. Until one day the time comes when he too finds the cage door open and with one final beat of the heart escapes from the inadequate.

From Zum Gedächtnis
(In Memoriam) *1916*

LITTLE SONG

Rainbow song in the rain
The magic of dying light
Joy like a sweet refrain
Fading in the night
The Madonna's face in pain
Life's bitter delight …

The wind that blasts the bloom
The wreath laid on the tomb
Pleasure all too brief.
Star to darkness hurled:
Veil of beauty and grief
Over the depths of the world.

AFTERWORD

Hermann Hesse was one of those artists fortunate enough to grow old, and thus be able to experience all phases of life and, in his inimitable fashion, to depict them. He was a man of complex and fragile temperament, who lived a life of intense creativity both as a writer and painter (the twenty volumes of his collected works comprise some 14,000 pages, his correspondence ran to about 35,000 letters, and he painted around 3,000 watercolours), and so the fact that he reached the age of eighty-five was something that could scarcely be taken for granted. Generally such gifts carry their own risks, and such intensity tends to shorten life expectancy. For the most part, those who deviate from the norm and go their own independent way encounter many obstacles and meet with much resistance from their fellow men, as a consequence of which their stay on earth tends to be far shorter than that of people who get along with the world 'as it is', and are able to adapt and indeed knuckle under to it. At least twice, when he tried to commit suicide at the age of fourteen and again later at forty-six during the crisis before he wrote *Der Steppenwolf*, it is far from certain that Hesse would have survived his depressions had it not been for chance and for certain people stepping in at the right moments to look after him.

The fact that apart from these inner conflicts he also survived external dangers—the historical traumas of the First World War and especially the threat of National Socialism—was due to his political farsightedness, which made him "the first voluntary emigrant" (Joachim Maass) as early as 1912, and from 1924 he was a Swiss citizen. Anyone who has read the diary-like self-revelations of his letters and has thus got to know his bitter opposition to the trends of his time cannot help but be continually astonished at how long he was able to maintain this conflict-laden existence, and also at the lack of bitterness in his works, which focus not on the turmoil of the age but on the often astonishing simplicity of purification and enlightenment.

Old age and maturity—as we see for ourselves every day—do not necessarily belong together. "People often become old, but rarely mature," wrote the French author Alphonse Daudet. Very few have the good fortune, despite physical decline, to maintain their inner flexibility and to extract from the restrictions of old age the serenity, tolerance and good-humoured open-mindedness that recapture the charm of youthful spontaneity. This needs a process of consciousness that Heinrich von Kleist described in his famous essay about the puppet theatre:

> *We see that in the degree to which … reflection becomes darker and weaker, grace (innocence) emerges ever more radiant and dominant. But just as when two lines intersect, one cuts through the endlessness of the other and suddenly finds itself on the other side, or the image in a concave mirror moves into the endless distance and then suddenly confronts us again, so too when knowledge has as it were passed through endlessness, grace emerges again—so that at the same time it appears at its purest [in someone] who has either no consciousness or endless consciousness.*

The ninety-one-year-old Pablo Picasso expressed the same thought rather more simply, though no less strikingly: "One needs to live long in order to become young." In the case of Hermann Hesse at any rate, what his first biographer Hugo Ball wrote of him is certainly true: "He felt old in his youth and young in his old age."

This volume begins with observations the author made when he was forty-three. These are impressions relating to spring, the rebirth and renewal of nature, depicted by a man at the halfway stage of his life, conscious of the fleeting transience of the world of appearances, into which he knew he was drawn and which he did not resist. The yearly repetition of life's regeneration does not give him cause to lament the fact that he himself is no longer at that same stage which makes spring so radiant and so full of joy and hope, but it spurs him into thinking about his own process of change and regeneration. He has long been aware of the relativity of youth and age:

"All gifted, differentiated people are old one minute and young the next, just as they're happy one minute and sad the next … But people are not always on a level with their own age—inwardly they often rush ahead, and even more frequently they lag behind; then their conscious mind and feeling for life are less mature than their body, they resist its natural manifestations, and demand from themselves something that they cannot achieve."

The vain struggle of a consciousness that grows younger from crisis to crisis against the decline of the body was all too familiar to Hermann Hesse. As a 'Man of Fifty', on the one hand he is in need of health cures, and on the other he is driven by such a lust for life that he even takes dancing lessons, spends his nights at masked balls, and watches himself with a kind of black humour, having long since seen through the vanity of such escapes. But only when he has lived out this revolt against the gradual fading of the body's joys and pleasures and has tested them to the full does he succeed in grasping comparable processes in the world around him. When, for example, after a storm the shadows emerge a little more sharply, objects lose their colour but take on a more defined shape, he takes this as an image for the process of ageing. Instead of bemoaning the loss of colour and sensuality, he relishes the gain in form and profile. And from there it is no great step to the realisation that "Age is not worse than youth; Lao Tse is not worse than Buddha. Blue is not worse than red." Age is only pathetic "when it wants to play at being young".

He becomes aware of more and more of the joyful aspects of age once he has given up fighting against it—the increased serenity that makes us less sensitive to blows and pinpricks, the reservoir of experiences, images and memories from the past, which—thanks to the benevolent selectivity of the memory—often seems more beautiful and more worthwhile than the present, the prospect of imminent liberation from the fragility of the body, and communion with all our friends, with people we love and respect and who have preceded us to death, and finally the fearful yet confident curiosity concerning what awaits us afterwards. As he writes at the end of his famous poem 'Stages':

Perhaps one day even the final knell
Will have yet more new rooms for us in store
And life will go on calling evermore …
And so, my heart, take leave and fare you well!

Anyone who in addition to these texts from four decades is also able to look into the soul revealed by photos of Hermann Hesse in his old age, the most impressive of which are those taken by his son Martin, will endorse the comment made by his fellow writer Ernst Petzoldt:

"The goal of all artistic endeavour is none other than to look in old age just as, for example, Hermann Hesse did. Indeed, I would say one doesn't even need to read him, but simply to look at him in order to be cognisant of his life and work. For his written character is absolutely identical to this ageless countenance, and represents the quintessence, so to speak, of all poems and writings. But we would not really see him without having read him!"

VOLKER MICHELS 1990

A BIOGRAPHICAL SKETCH

Hermann Hesse was born on the second of July 1877 in Calw, Württenberg. His father was a Protestant missionary from Estonia and his mother the daughter of a Württemberg Indologist, and they had first met at a mission in India. His grandfather Hermann Gundert ran a publishing house in Calw, and his large library was at the disposal of the avid young reader. In 1891 Hesse was sent to the Seminary at Maulbronn Abbey, which he mentions in the passage entitled *Autumnal Experiences*, but he ran away, and after bitter conflicts with his parents he tried to commit suicide in May 1892.

By working in a bookshop in Tübingen, Hesse became financially independent, and in 1898 he published a small volume of poetry called *RomantischeLieder* (Romantic Songs), followed in 1899 by a novella called *Eine Stunde hinter Mitternacht* (One Hour After Midnight). Both works were failures. In 1900, he was rejected for military service because of eye trouble and this, together with various nervous disorders, was to plague him throughout his life. The novel *Peter Camenzind*, published in 1904 by Samuel Fischer, was a major breakthrough, and from then on he was able to live on his writing.

In 1904 he married Marie Bernoulli, and they lived in Gaienhofen on Lake Constance, where she bore him three sons. It was here that Hesse renewed his earlier interest in Buddhism and theosophy—an interest which was to lead much later to one of his most famous works, *Siddhartha* (1922). However, his marriage was soon in difficulties, and a long trip to Sri Lanka and Indonesia, followed by the family's move to Bern, Switzerland, in 1912 did not help matters. During the First World War, as a staunch pacifist he made many enemies in Germany by publishing an essay attacking nationalism, and his personal crisis deepened when in 1916 his father died, his son Martin became very ill, and his wife's schizophrenia became a matter of serious concern. His own mental condition deteriorated, and he had to undergo psychiatric treatment.

By 1919, the marriage had broken down irretrievably, and Hesse moved to Ticino, where he rented rooms in Montagnola. In 1924 he married the singer Ruth Wenger, but this marriage also broke down. By now he was a naturalised Swiss citizen, and shortly after the publication and worldwide success of his novel *Steppenwolf*, he married Ninon Dolbin, née Ausländer, an art historian. In 1931 he designed the Casa Hesse, near Montagnola, where he was to spend the rest of his life.

He observed the rise of the Nazis with great concern, and in 1933 helped Bertolt Brecht and Thomas Mann on their journeys into exile. He was bitterly opposed to anti-Semitism (his third wife was Jewish), and eventually his work was banned in Nazi Germany. In 1946 he was awarded the Nobel Prize for Literature, and although he continued to write stories, reviews and poems, he devoted much of his remaining time to painting watercolours and attending to a vast correspondence. He died in his sleep of a brain haemorrhage on the ninth of August 1962, and is buried in Montagnola at the San Abbondio cemetery.

Volker Michels has calculated that Hesse's literary works comprise some 14,000 pages, while he wrote about 35,000 letters, and painted about 3,000 watercolours. He once talked of his "lifelong failure to acquire a talent for idleness".

DHW 2011

ABOUT THIS EDITION

This English translation is based on the Insel Taschenbuch 2857, which is an extended and revised version of Insel Taschenbuch 2311—Hermann Hesse, *Mit der Reife wird man immer jünger, Betrachtungen und Gedichte über das Alter*, edited by Volker Michels (Frankfurt am Main and Leipzig—Insel Verlag, 1990). The poems have been taken from the edition—Hermann Hesse, *Die Gedichte* (Frankfurt am Main 1977). For extracts from novels and longer passages, the source and date of publication are given at the end of each text. The shorter texts are taken mainly from Hermann Hesse's letters.